Upwinds

UPWINDS

A short report on spiritual upwinds
in our time

by Anders Otterland
and Lennart Sunnergren

THOMAS NELSON INC., PUBLISHERS
NASHVILLE   NEW YORK

Originally published in Swedish as *Uppvindar,* copyright 1973 Den
Kristna Bokringen, Stockholm

LIBRARY OF CONGRESS CATALOGING IN PUBLICATION DATA
Otterland, Anders, 1920-
    Upwinds

    Translation of *Uppvindar.*

    1. Pentecostalishm. I. Sunnergren, Lennart, 1930- joint author.
II. Title.
BX8763.08713   248'.2   75-14367
ISBN 0-8407-5599-6

CONTENTS

PART I   BACKGROUND

     1. The Singing in the Marketplace   9

     2. Upwinds   16

PART II   THE DATA: POPULATION AND ENVIRONMENT

     3. The Chapel   23

     4. Thousands of Prayer Groups   34

     5. Sunday   46

     6. Open House for Bible Studies   55

     7. A Continuous Bible Study in a Home   62

     8. A Usual Weekday Evening or an Unusual   77

     9. We All Need Help Sometimes   93

     10. "Ye Shall Be Witnesses"   101

PART III   A CRUDE ANALYSIS OF DATA

11. Social and Other Characteristics
    of Charismatics Supported by
    Examples   115

PART IV   COMMENTS

12. The First Day of Pentecost   137

13. The Second Day of Pentecost   140

14. Questions and Answers in
    Summary   147

P. S. WARM WINDS OF LOVE

PART I

Background

CHAPTER 1

The Singing in the Marketplace

"We are one in the Spirit. We are one in the Lord. And they'll know we are Christians by our love, by our love. Yes, they'll know . . ."

The words of this Lutheran song echo out over the marketplace of an old, old Swedish town on a sunny, mild summer morning. Flowers, fruits, and vegetables in every combination and color one could dream of are on display in the market stands and tables. Business is brisk, but it slows for a moment or two as people stop and listen intently and willingly to the singing. Some even join in the singing as more songs follow. The songs are about happiness in God and Oneness through the Holy Spirit. The close fellowship expressed in the singing is unmistakable. It is so real!

Four generations are listening and singing there in the market among the vegetable stands, just as they have for years on market day. Not only the "usual" churchgoers are singing, but people in general. The oldest are sitting on the benches around the monument with its water fountain flowing just behind them. The middle-aged and young adults are standing in a semicircle around the singers forming a sort of choir. The babies and toddlers are sleeping in their carriages or sitting on their daddies' shoulders or pushing their way to the very front to really see and take in all

9

that is going on. Even the teen-agers have stopped their whispering and laughing among themselves and are now listening intently.

The choir consists of about twenty teen-agers. Three musicians have joined them today. Two play guitars and the third an organ. All the instruments are connected to amplifiers.

The "choir director" is a young girl, who plans to be a schoolteacher. But this year she is "giving full-time to the Lord" in her home church as a "youth leader" and "outreach worker." Now she is leading the singing with such enthusiasm that others are moved to join her in this inspiring, outgoing singing. The amplifier carries the words of the song all across the square, down the small narrow streets, and into the little old houses that form the center of this town's oldest sector. In the café close by one can see people listening to the singing through the open windows as they enjoy their "eleven o'clock" morning coffee. And at the police station at one end of the square the officers have opened the windows and are standing in them to listen.

A young man, so tall that one can see him easily among all the others, now comes forward to one of the microphones. He is another "youth leader" in the church. With a clear voice he quotes a verse from the Bible about God's love. In his talk he urges his listeners not to lose the opportunity to receive this love. It is a free gift through the Holy Spirit! It is obvious that the people are listening to what he has to say.

The girl who leads the singing comes forward again and gathers her little choir together. Then she turns to one of the microphones and says, "This time we are going to sing a song with 'movements' to it. It is a song about Jesus and His love for us. This love is as deep as an ocean, as high as the mountains, and as broad as the horizon." By moving

10

her arms she signifies the height, length, and depths of this love. The choir sings the song again and again. Many out in the crowd join them. A few even try to do the arm movements. When they do it wrong, they laugh from the bottom of their hearts. The oneness in the marketplace is unmistakable.

Among the "choir" members is a young man who is about 20 years old. A year ago he was one of many who had experienced "the charismatic renewal" in a Christian conference. For the first time in his life he then had perceived "the reality" in Jesus Christ. He had "personally met Jesus," whom he from that day on had followed.

The boy now reflects this. Every day he now realizes that his Master's revolutionary teachings of love between people form the only worthwhile program for a victorious life. He knows what he is singing about, because he saw His love with his own eyes in the people changed by its message. Yes, "Jesus and His love are Wonderful!"

"How beautifully they sing," an old lady among the listeners whispers. She looks at her nearest neighbor, who is standing and watching, just as she is.

This neighbor nods back that she is very right, and in her broad country accent she whispers, "Yes, and so tremendously happy and nice they look. I hope that somebody takes a picture."

We, the authors of this book, were also at the marketplace that brilliant, early summer day. We belong to two different generations of town life. There is nearly a quarter of a century between us. Certainly enough to give us different perspectives! Both of us were born in this town and have been influenced by its deep religious life and the constant warmth and renewal in the church and chapel. Both of us have social interests, and our university studies made us still more interested in researching the social and medical impact of this constant flow of warm religion, not only in the lives of individual people within this one town, but in society at large.

For generations the people in this town, which is located between two horizontal mountains, have been moved by the Gospel. The first Swedish king to become a Christian was baptized in a well on another matching mountain not very far away. The distinctive profile of this mountain is clearly visible about thirty miles northwest of town on any clear day. The churches are many on the plateau of farmland between the mountains. The oldest churches are round and date back to the era when early Christians had to defend themselves against outsiders. The mighty teachings of the church have followed the people of this vast farmland generation after generation for centuries.

Most of the churches in the town find that now, as always, people are crowding to their services. In addition, in the last two or three years a special renewal has been noted. People talk about a new religious awakening, about an outpouring of the Spirit, that more than any other has reached many churches and denominations in many countries at the same time. Yes, an awakening and an outpouring of God's Spirit all over the world! One talks about a "new revival—a revival of dimensions never before seen. Many have called this phenomenon "a charismatic awakening" after the Greek word "charisma," which means a divine gift. In other words, the gifts of the Spirit of the Lord are functioning and in evidence in people's lives in churches as seldom seen before.

We wanted to know more about the people in this revival. We wanted to know what happened to them the day after their first day of renewal: how they were functioning on their *second day and all the following days.*

This new movement was very similar to the spiritual atmosphere in which we had grown up and the fruits of which we had always enjoyed. We had seen how people were changed spiritually as well as socially in the vineyard of the church. We had seen men and women grow into pillars in the church, responsible citizens, and even into positions of public office.

We had one baseline: "a congregation," about which we "knew everything," a congregation of which we were a part from our childhood, and our parents before us since they were young, a congregation born out of a renewal when the century was young, a congregation that we knew and loved.

What were the signs of the renewal? What caused its "epidemic" development? What caused the sudden growth of activity in so many churches and denominations at the same time? What caused the enthusiastic renewal of Christian brothers and sisters, who were testifying to richer "Spiritual experiences," the "Gifts of the Spirit in action," and the "Fruits of the Spirit" here and now? How did this renewal come about? What changes in individual lives had followed in the steps of this movement? How does this revival manifest itself today in people's lives? Are the consequences of this renewal, these warm winds of love, the same as those we had seen before?

In order to get intelligent answers to as many of our many questions as possible, we worked up a questionnaire which, at random, we asked people in the movement to answer. We also used questions from this questionnaire when talking to people who had experienced a renewal in their lives. We came to know all of these personalities by name. In our own report, however, we were not to mention any names, with a few exceptions. No fictitious names were given. The testimonies were to be presented just as they were. We hoped that perhaps the readers of the report would identify themselves in one or more of the many situations from real life about which this deals and receive the same amount of blessing.

To measure changes of medical-chemical nature taking

place when a drug addict, for instance, claims a religious conversion is as difficult to do as what the individual testifies to feeling in such events: feelings which these people describe as "streams of living water," "peace surpassing all understanding," and "happiness knowing no limitations." However, a descriptive measure of the social effects of these experiences seems plausible.

This is a fully acceptable measurement: If a person who earlier did not function in his studies, in his job, as a family member or with his fellow man suddenly starts doing so, this change, this difference, could be accepted as a measurement which could even be graded. For instance, if a person who previously had to be supported now needs no help, that fact would be a sign of a change. If somebody now can give instead of only receive, then rehabilitation is presumably in most cases even further on its way. If somebody who was previously caring so little about himself that he obviously, while knowing better, impaired his health suddenly wakes up and starts caring about himself and others, then something worth noting has taken place. If someone previously could not fulfill even simple criteria of mental-emotional health and now fulfills these, it is obvious that a healing process is under way. The criteria we decided to use were:

1. The ability to receive and give love.
2. The ability to take responsibility.
3. The ability to be loving.
4. The ability to do something productive.*

The dramatic conversion is always fascinating, so also is the silent and less dramatic. The charismatic movement has an abundance of testimonies about changes in people's lives. The activities of these spiritual people are vivid and vital,

---

*This broad definition of emotional well-being was also used by John P. Kihldahl in his study *The Psychology of Speaking in Tongues,* New York, 1972.

and history of this revival is written in many ways through their lives.

Thus, through our questionnaire, we interviewed either in person or in writing individuals who testified to having had the charismatic experience. We also attended many services, many different services! And we were invited to people's homes for prayer meetings and Bible studies. It is about that which we saw and heard as eyewitnesses and read through our questionnaires that this report deals. It is, we believe, a documentation of what is going on right now. It does not deal with theological discussions, because these people don't care about such things anymore. No, this report deals with real changes, here and now, in people's lives, changes nobody can deny, changes through the Gospel, the Love, of Jesus Christ. It deals with "Oneness in the Spirit," just as they were singing about and experiencing that beautiful morning in the Swedish marketplace, when the idea to "take pictures" of all this started to grow.

It is with these pictures that this report deals.

CHAPTER 2

Upwinds

Normally, on the vast farmland at home around and between the unruffled mountains, it is quite windy: a productive and unusual wind. Both winter and summer, autumn and spring, the wind is almost always there—sometimes just a little tiny breeze, and sometimes like a gale.

The wind blows the snow in drifts in the wintertime, and during the summertime the heads of grain float themselves strong and big in the wind and sing like the waves of an ocean.

When autumn comes, the harvest of wheat, rye, and oats gets dry in the wind; and in the spring, the wind prepares the fields for the plowing.

High above all this, the clouds sail. They are always airy and broken in pieces by the wind—pieces of art at which one likes to look.

So it was many years ago, and so it will be again. Haze and fog and dark heavy clouds will not have a chance! Why? Because when the winds from the vast farmlands meet the mountains, they progress on up the slopes and continue upward, up into the air to break all the overcast, heavy clouds. Upwinds! On these upwinds the gliders sail high above the farmland. They are even able to fly on the wind toward goals far, far away!

Today the winds of the Holy Spirit are flowing all over

the world. These winds are stronger than they ever were. We certainly live in the times of the upwinds!

Parents of many misled young people have been pressed down under the constant uncertainty and capriciousness of the paranoid features (feeling of being observed, hunted) in the poison-and-provocation-filled drug culture. Separated or divorced husbands and wives have felt the distress of one another and their children and families. Children and teenagers grieve at their friends' and brothers' and sisters' drifting around like lost ships. All these concerned people have joined the many faithful, anonymous, prayerful sisters and brothers of the church and "sought the throne of Grace" as never before. The prayers have formed holy mountains of hope at the horizon.

The distress in the world has become more and more compounded as personal tragedies are more and more obvious. Like dark heavy clouds this distress has darkened the day.

But now the upwinds of the Holy Spirit are ripping apart the dark clouds! One can see the sun! And one can fly again!! Broken people, who thought they did not even have wings, have gotten new feathers with which to fly. They have received new wings which again carry them! People who were pressed down by sorrow and failure experience again the happiness of victory. Runaways have acquired the power to return home. Parents now have time for their children and others, and children have time for their parents and other older people. All have discovered time to worship and relax together, to just sit down and listen. People have found their way back home. People who had not been functioning for a long time are functioning again. "God is so great and I am glad that in His grace He found me once again," one sings. And one says, "Thank you, Lord, for letting me fly. Thank you, Lord, for upwinds divine. Thank you, Lord, for letting me live. Thank you for all the abundance you give."

"Thank you, Lord, for my new wings, which carried me home!"

With expressions like these, people praise God for the religious awakening, which at the present time is reaching all corners of the world.

Let us immediately give an example of what we are trying to describe. Let us offer you just now a little taste of what we plan to relate in this book.

He was a young man rushing around making a fool of himself and others when God changed him into a responsible, functioning member of his world through the upwinds of the Holy Spirit. He is one of many we plan to introduce to you. One of many, many more we have met during this last year. What happened to this young man and all these others, women and men, young and old, is impossible to explain and to find words for without using "religious terms" or "the language of Canaan." We have accepted these expressions as adequate in describing an "inner" happening, suitable because what has happened with people "religiously," "in their hearts," in "their inner beings" has had astonishing "external" consequences.

He was a floating, troubled twenty-year-old boy, always hunting happiness. He was looking for happiness in intoxication, extremely loud music, cars, and roaring gangs of boys and girls. Of course there were moments of real fellowship, but these moments were short. Most of these people only egotistically took whatever was available. One exploited the other! Therefore, also, this young man became more and more dishonest. All the explanations! The obvious lies! Unreal false fabrications without actuality! He was not able to complete one little thing. He rushed away from everything unfinished. He thought he was big when he was stoned by alcohol, marijuana, or some other drug, and when he lied for his girlfriends. He did not conquer one single "temptation." He didn't want to be like that, but not one promise to stop what he was doing to himself was he able to keep. It was impossible for him to change himself. Everything became more and more complicated. The police and also his "friends" were always after him. But he refused to realize the consequences of this. Short hours of "skin" satisfaction were followed by deeper reactive depressions and feelings of being a total failure, which it took wilder and wilder orgies to only temporarily overcome. He was in an evil circle from which he could not exit.

After a long series of unusual circumstances, he was invited one Saturday noon to a lunch for young people. This lunch was part of a meeting organized by a local chapter of The Full Gospel Businessmen's Fellowship International. As a matter of fact this lunch meeting turned out to be the most important event in his entire life. The meeting was long, followed by an even longer prayer meeting. But to him it was short!

The young man told us afterward what happened. The program included singing, "testimonies," and an address by an especially invited speaker. Everything was real, down to earth, and living, he felt. He had never earlier either seen or heard anything like it. During the address, for the first time in his young life, he saw face to face the truth about himself—the whole truth about a whole man. Up until that time he had only been a body, with which he egotistically rushed around and hunted desire. Now he realized that he also had a religious part within him, a part which, until that time, he had totally neglected.

After the sermon, a final hymn of invitation was sung. During the hymn singing something happened to the boy. He lifted his hands as a spontaneous, unexpected expression of a strong, inner scream of freedom. In reality, he cried out his total surrender. In that moment of honesty about himself, his body was filled with some unexplainable warmth. The heavy pressure, which had burdened him, was lifted away. He was completely engulfed with peace, peace without any boundaries. The happiness that he felt was unlimited, and he expressed all this in a language which was not his own! It subconsciously came to him, and although he could scarcely believe that this was happening, it was true!

This meeting became the turning point in this boy's life, and afterwards he started to function! People came and asked what had happened to him. Since he did not have to search around anymore, he now had time for things he had never before had time to do: meet people and talk with them in a relaxed manner, stay home many good long evenings, read the Bible from start to end, pray, and just relax. He discovered very much which he had seldom seen or heard before—nature's wonders, the birds' singing, and many other beautiful things.

His mind cleared up, and his studies became meaningful and successful. He saw everything in a new way.

More than a year has passed since the remarkable youth luncheon. One cannot recognize the boy either by behavior or looks. His basic personality is the same, but now he seems to be filled with harmony. He is calm, satisfied, happy, and knows what he wants. He is detoxified. Beautifully detoxified! One who had had his head completely occupied by hallucinations now has visions about himself and others—visions about being a part of building a new land through a message of rebirth into peace and forgiveness between people, a message about a new love between peoples and countries, a message which Jesus Christ with a few words summarized:

"A new commandment I give unto you, that ye love one another; as I have loved you, that ye also love one another" (John 13:34).

New "feathers in his wings" gave him power to fly. He was lifted up by the upwinds of the Holy Spirit! Upwinds! Warm winds of love!!

PART II

The Data:
Population and Environment

CHAPTER 3

The Chapel

"We are one in the Spirit, we are one in the Lord. We are one in the Spirit, we are one in the Lord. And they'll know we are Christians by our love, by our love. Yes, they'll know we are Christians by our love."

The same Lutheran song. The same genuine fellowship. The same feeling of being "one in the Spirit." Only the place is another. Instead of a service in a marketplace in a small town in Sweden, a service coordinated by an old, old church, we are attending a prayer meeting in a house in a big city in the U.S.A. For just about a year this house has been the center of many prayer groups in that city.

The house is a big mansion located on a beautiful park-like lot. The house has many large rooms and hallways. There is space for some three hundred persons in these big prayer meetings, where people from all church denominations and social strata come together. The place has received the nickname, "The Chapel." And that is what we will call it, "The Chapel."

It is almost perceptible how the Chapel gets filled with fellowship and love during the singing. All are participating. All are one in the Spirit. Again and again they sing, "We are one in the Spirit, we are one in the Lord."

During the singing some people lift their hands in praises to the Lord as they are thanking God for this deep, close communion which nobody can deny, even if its nature is difficult to explain.

The singing continues into a prayer, a joint prayer. All join hands. Like a big family one carries one another's burdens. A strong feeling of togetherness fills every corner of the house. "We are one in the Spirit. We are one in the Lord."

SOME PERSONALITIES IN THE CHAPEL

The prayers are led by a man in his early forties, called Brother Bill. His forefathers were of great dignity—Cherokees. One clearly notices his Indian heritage. His entire person radiates physical and spiritual force, marked with vivid and open alertness. The prayer testifies to strong faith and tender empathy. He cries with all these brothers and sisters, his brothers and sisters in the Lord, as he wipes the tears from his dark Indian eyes.

He opens his eyes now and looks around. People continue to pray. He takes in all this, just as we do, from the middle of "the scene." It is only to register the picture: with lifted hands in earnest praises the sixty-year-old general—now a practicing lawyer—stands singing and praying with his eyes closed and his face turned "towards heaven." His suit is spotless. His tie clasp matches his cufflinks. Only three years ago he "surrendered himself to the Lord" during a revival in the city. Some time later, according to his own testimony, he was "baptized in the Holy Spirit."

The general says that after he "had lost his entire life before," and "had been cheated of the real values in life," he then became intensely eager to study this new reality through the Bible. The person of Jesus fascinated him. On broad rolls of paper he wrote down the family tree of Jesus. Ministers and others have found this family tree so interesting and accurate that the general is very busy these days as a speaker in churches and clubs on the topic of Jesus. Of

24

course, for the general, Jesus is no longer merely a historic personality. He is also his Lord and Saviour.

The general's wife looks at her husband with tears in her eyes. Her turquoise dress somehow matches the blue-green of her eyes and her dark hair with a streak of gray. She has also been touched by this remarkable renewal, and her testimony has taken her to many a rostrum.

Now they stand here side by side with a boy with long, long hair. The boy is dressed in boots, torn jeans, a shirt which has never been touched by a tie, and an old, old jacket. It is not very long since this young man was helplessly involved in drugs, involved until he met Jesus. Jesus set him free. With eyes radiating deep happiness he whispers, "Thank you, Jesus." The lawyer looks at him and says the same words and probably thinks: it is good to know that a lawyer's clients seek help and strength at the throne of the strongest of all—the Lord—the only one who can keep this boy strong and clean, whole and free. "Thank you, Jesus."

A twenty-seven-year-old man, foreman in a cooperative farm company, also joins hands with the boy standing next to the general and his wife. During his military service this man had been a sergeant. He knows what it takes to deal with young boys and the types of communication difficulties one can anticipate between officers and privates. He looks and he smiles when he sees this sight. Beautiful! Only a year ago he would not have felt so! Tough and hard to start with, he had worked at being even tougher by drinking and secretly taking drugs. The poison from alcohol and other chemical preparations foreign to biological life made him sick and depressed. But on the verge of suicide he accepted Christ through his wife's testimony. He became a totally new man in no time. His attitude toward people changed from a hard critic to a loving big brother. God sanctified his talent for leadership and appointed him to be an elder, full of wisdom. Now he studies to become a minister. His young family is one of the most charming we have ever met.

Over there an elderly lady is standing. She wears expensive and fashionable clothing, with a fitting coiffure, and there is an air of pleasant perfume around her. She prays loudly about blessings for herself and her neighbor on the next chair. Her neighbor is also a well-dressed lady in her fifties or sixties. She has publicly asked for prayer to be free from an alcoholic addiction. She had been drinking secretly, but does not do this anymore, for she does not need "artificial euphoria." She is here experiencing "natural euphoria," for which she is praising the Lord. Besides, she is not feeling lonely anymore. In the Chapel she has got an abundance of sisters and brothers. One "sister," for instance, is holding her arms around her shoulders. This lady is always willing to help, always full of empathy and with a ready smile on her face, despite deep tragedies of her own. What a deaconess! All these ladies are so beautiful in their honesty and their ease before God. It is impossible to describe this scene in words!

In the same row we notice a young also alone and divorced mother. She is very poor but very relaxed in her happiness in God. Not far from her a slightly gray-haired, well-dressed beautiful lady wearing glasses and in her fifties is sitting. In a short period of time she has come into a very active life in the kingdom of the Lord from earlier having labored with metaphysical questions. At her side stands her husband, a tall dark-haired forceful man, now praising the Lord with closed eyes. They have a classical dancer to their left. She, also, has chosen the Chapel as her house of prayer. She had successfully traveled about ten years with well-established theatrical companies. Later, she married a producer. Everything seemed to be all right when tragic circumstances left her alone with a small girl. In her agony she sought God. For months a missionary she did not know

26

had been praying for her, that she might find "the right way" for her life. She found "the way," and now we see her here full of devotion and deeply engaged in the most beautiful part she ever played: worshipping the Lord for salvation through Jesus Christ.

Also, a fifty-five-year-old mason is participating in this prayer meeting. His broad shoulders, his strong arms and hands, and his eyes filled with a new morning indicate stability. He radiates quality and authority. With his arms stretched upwards he is now standing in front of "The Holy One," as one waiting to be used by God. It had taken many years and great humiliation before he had come so far. As a honored member during many years in unions and other organizations, he had seen the worth of being considered in an earthly "good standing." He really was a big man in these relations, but it did not give him power to live a victorious life. This became a possibility just after he had experienced "the baptism in the Holy Spirit." This experience gave the strong mason entirely new possibilities and dimensions in serving through his talents to speak and be a leader. He thus became an important tool in building up the church consisting of bricks of people. He became one of the most talented and outstanding Bible study leaders in the city!! He became a man who constantly prayed—especially for the sick—and, as a "preacher-prophet," a humble instrument in God's hands.

A physician with a chairmanship on an important committee in the medical society in his city also stands here with lifted hands, praying, praising God, and singing. His fifty years and professional experience had gotten a halo of harmony here "close to God." He holds out one hand toward his neighbor's, a young schoolteacher who has had the privilege of living with Christ for a while. She had recently been appointed by her schoolboard to a very unique job. Now she is praising the Lord for this opportunity and asking Him to give her wisdom for this new challenge. Both are singing, "We are one in the Spirit, we are one in the Lord," and look around thankfully and full of wonder.

They see, as we do, a little bit further towards the front the many young people, girls and boys, students at the colleges and universities. They know that none of these, in reality, functioned before. But they function now and only since recently, when they "through Christ Jesus met God." They are just "babies" in the faith and are sitting there "praising God" wholeheartedly. Nowhere during their years of studies, often including one or a couple of so-called sabbatical years, have they met a more real fellowship. Here they are important people; they are sisters and brothers, all related in God's kingdom—the dancer, the mason, the general, the sergeant and the private, the physician, the students, the professors, the singers, the older women and the young, the older men and the young, the blacks, the whites and the reds, the professionally educated and the blue collar workers, the rich and the poor, grandmothers and children, fathers and mothers and unmarried young people asking God for guidance in their lives. All are one, with no generation gap, no social boundaries, no racial limitations, no hair or beard or clothing barricades. All are equal before the Lord. There are no accusations about who was at fault, who was to blame for failures. All admit they have been wrong. At last they all have been able to honestly say, "Forgive me, I am to blame." All know that without a teamwork between "spirit, body, and soul" no one has any chance at all. After one's earlier starved "religious being," now beginning to "eat" balanced food has caused everything to become so very much healthier among all. All are sisters and brothers, parents and children—God's children. Yes, all have become members of the family of the Kingdom of the Lord. Brothers! Sisters! Women, who for the first time in their adult lives have felt that they are loved and cared for just because they are people, are now "flowering" in the presence of the Lord into a beauty which no miracle treatments of this world could ever have produced—the pure clean beauty of people who know within that they are new creations in Christ Jesus. "The old is gone, and something new has come into their lives." They can frankly lift their eyes because "their sins are forgiven." Brothers and sisters who are all willing to try to understand one another, willing to start anew themselves, and willing to admit their errors and to forgive seventy times seven.

The Chapel has a special atmosphere conducive to "spiritual experiences." Why? It is always filled with people praying and praising the Lord. How did this charismatic place of fellowship come about? We will let Brother Bill answer the question. He saw this renewal grow in the city. "It started about one and a half years ago," he says. "Some friends from one of the many prayer groups in the city asked me, because I am a minister, to come and lead Bible studies with them, which I did. My own church had nothing against this. The prayer group to which I was invited had been meeting in a home every Tuesday evening. All in the group were new converts, and now they asked me to come regularly every week for continuous Bible studies. It looked like the hunger after God's Word was never satisfied. The group consisted at the beginning of seven or eight men and women.

"At about this same time we started to ask ourselves in our church how we could best be of a blessing for all these many in the new wave of religious awakening. As a matter of fact, there were many people in this revival quite different from what we were used to. The new ones formed a beautiful mixture of people with long hair and no profession at all, well-known businessmen, people with university degrees and established professions, blacks and whites, singing stars, Catholics and others from the old churches, and many, many more. All these people needed love and understanding, Bible studies, prayers, and counseling.

"The Tuesday evening prayer group grew and grew with people who for the first time saw Christians in action. This group became somewhat of a rescue station for many, not least for people from the "upper social circles," and at the same time from the bottom, and all between.

"One of the ladies who came to the Tuesday evening prayer group invited some time later the group to have prayer meetings in her home—a mansion in which she had grown up. This place had been vacant some time for repairs. There was plenty of room and more and more people came to the prayer meetings, and many more were converted and renewed and experienced God, the Holy Spirit.

"From that time on, several other prayer groups all over the city asked me to come and lead Bible studies with them on a regular basis every week," Brother Bill continues. "The Lord spoke to me and guided me into this more and more, and I felt that this was His will that I should give very much time to this special work. An entirely new mission field had opened up for us in the midst of our city and among people whom we never thought that we would reach. We thought that these people were forever to remain indifferent to the message. But we soon realized that they had as deep religious needs as the rest of us. Their eagerness to testify about their new experiences, salvation, and baptism in the Holy Spirit did not know any limitations and explains very much the tremendous growth of this renewal. But, as is indicated previously, these people were entirely new for us. There were more persons with academic degrees and higher positions and better off than we usually reached and at the same time more 'poor,' more who had problems with drugs and

alcohol, more from other 'ethnic groups.' In every city, in
every community, one can find such mission fields with
ripe harvests. The hunger to know more about God's Word
among all these really is great. I felt guided to resign from
my position as pastor in a church to be able to work full-
time as counselor and Bible teacher on this new field. My
parishioners, as well as my colleagues among the ministers,
supported me one hundred percent and understood when
I told them how I felt when considering this call. I needed
their prayers. And, carried on these prayers with happiness
and assurance, I went to serve in this new and, for us,
totally unusual work! In our regular meetings in the city
for ministers my colleagues always want to hear about us,
and we always pray that the Lord will give strength to be
just workers who are eager to harvest these quickly ripening
fields.

"The work, which the Lord thus gave us, was an answer
to prayers. My entire life I had wanted to be able to really
give full time to Bible studies, counseling, and prayers,
and to have only a minimum of administrative work.
Administrative work does not take most of my time anymore. This last year has been the most different and the
most rewarding of my twenty-five years as a minister of the
Gospel. Now I teach in about fifteen prayer groups every
week besides teaching in the Chapel. Because of the nature
of the prayer groups, I meet many persons every week
whom I have not met before and would not have reached
otherwise. My calling as a minister has gotten wider
dimensions.

"The prayer group in the Chapel now meets three times
a week: Tuesday evening, Sunday morning, and Sunday
evening. The house is filled almost every time we meet. But
it is not the same people who come every time. Some folks
work some evenings or are out serving the Lord in other
meetings. Out of the ones who come Sunday mornings about

half also come Sunday evenings and only about one third also come Tuesdays. Few are at all the meetings at the Chapel. Considering all this, week after week we reach about six hundred persons, who pray together in spirit, pray across all borderlines of churches and denominations. Most of the ones coming are newly converted, or have recently "experienced the charismatic renewal," or are praying for more blessing in this constantly ongoing renewal. As many as about sixty-five to seventy percent have "come to the Lord" during the last two years. All are hungry for the Word of God. On the Lord's calling by grace, I became a teacher for all these at a very ripe point of time.

"In a similar way the Lord called others to work in the prayer groups in our city. There are many lay preachers and Bible study leaders among the people at the Chapel. Among the young people who have been converted in our fellowship, for instance, already about fifteen have been called by the Lord to the ministry of the Gospel. These are all attending Bible colleges at the present time to be ready for the ministry!

"When one sees all these new persons from all churches and denominations together praising the Lord for what has taken place in their lives and in many others all over the city, one experiences almost word by word the content of the song, 'We are one in the Spirit, we are one in the Lord,'" Brother Bill sums up.

The authors of this book attended gatherings at the Chapel and at other prayer groups and Bible studies during a long period of time. We were well accepted, and we were able to see and hear and be part of the love and the fellowship of these people. In our entire lives we had been around church people at home and abroad. So we had a rich background for an overview. It was striking to us to see people from different epochs and from such different environments geographically, socially, and culturally give expression to their religious lives in such very similar ways, and how their experiences of the Lord changed and influenced people's lives exactly the same way as we had seen all those years back home.

We felt that these observations were worth being closely photographed, developed, and studied.

CHAPTER 4

Thousands of Prayer Groups

She has had a quite difficult time recently. In fact, a very difficult time—constant assault from her divorced husband. She would ask the authorities to step in, but she does not want to do this because of the children. She cannot take this heavy burden anymore, so today she asks her sisters and brothers in the prayer group to pray for her.

They gather around her, women of all ages. The youngest are about twenty years of age, and the oldest about sixty. Several come closer and lay their hands on her shoulders. Others stand a little bit further out in the circle, with heads and hands lifted upwards. Someone is praying loudly, others silently; and then all join together in a united prayer. The lady who is prayed for feels the sincere love of her sisters. At first, she cries because of distress and loneliness. Then she sheds tears of happiness and thankfulness: happiness because of friends with whom to share her troubles, thankfulness because of the privilege of being able to go to God together with friends and leave all her needs in the powerful hands of the Lord, thankfulness also for feeling God's presence despite unfortunate circumstances. Several of the ladies who surrounded her also wipe tears from their eyes. Everybody feels a "touch of God's Holy Spirit."

This scene is from a charismatic prayer group—one of thousands which have grown up during the last few years.

One finds them all over the world today, and recently, we have witnessed similar scenes many times. Thoughtfulness about one another and the ability to lift one another's burdens in love before "the throne of God" are undoubtedly nothing exceptional for this one prayer group. It is commonplace today—something that happens daily in this remarkable revival.

The prayer group, where these pictures were taken, started about a year ago. Most of the new interdenominational charismatic prayer groups have been in existence for a year or two, few more than three years. But there are also some "old prayer groups" which have been in operation for many years. These are more traditional and often form a part of just one church and its programs. The new ones have been born because neighbors and friends who earlier met to drink tea, for cocktails, or for card parties now instead meet regularly for prayers. Ten to fifteen participants is usually the highest number at any time. In some prayer groups, however, the number has increased to thirty or forty when the attendance is really good. Many attend more than one prayer group, and some as many as three or four weekly.

New people come almost every time, as one or more in the group bring somebody whom they have led to the Lord recently. Some of the visitors may come "to study" because they want to start a prayer group in their own home, and now they want to know how to go about it. This constant flow of people gives the advantage of a prayer group never becoming a "closed club" just for certain people. Anybody is welcome to participate. Many become so fascinated the first time they come—about what they see and hear—that they start a prayer group in their home as soon as possible by inviting their neighbors and friends. Through this eagerness the revival reaches out as never before. The first few times a new prayer group meets, an experienced layman or laywoman from another prayer group is quite often invited to testify about their experiences

THE PRAYER GROUPS HAVE
DIFFERENT PROFILES

The prayer groups have different profiles. There are groups which emphasize Bible studies under the guidance of a person with special knowledge of the Word of God. They study, for instance, one after another of the books of the Bible, systematically taking up one or two chapters each time. Others have perhaps chosen for study a special subject, such as the "Holy Spirit." Sometimes someone in the group brings tapes from Bible studies recorded by well-known Bible teachers. Entire Bible study series on tape may thus be covered in the program for a prayer group in time.

You will also find "pure" prayer groups in which praying forms the main part of the getting together. To share "what God has done" and "what God is doing day by day" in short testimonies is usual in all types of prayer groups.

Everybody who comes to prayer meetings does not testify to a charismatic experience. But all seem "open for all of God's gifts." They pray naturally and in a relaxed manner for one another to be able to receive whatever God has in store for them. The experiences of "the Baptism in the Holy Spirit" and the continuous "walking with the Lord" have become natural. There are many examples of this: A prayer meeting was almost over when a young girl, who was home from school on her Christmas vacation, asked the participants to pray for her. She wanted to be "filled with the Spirit" in the same beautiful way which her mother had experienced some time ago. Many of the participants "laid hands" on her and prayed. In that moment the girl felt an inner peace impossible to explain. When she tried to form what she felt into words, she spoke in a language she had never studied. It just came to her naturally—a language no one had taught her how to speak. The entire thing was new to her, and it was impossible to explain! The feeling of happiness "welled" forward from her "inner self." With this new dimension of happiness she went back to her university, testified to her friends, and gathered them together to pray. Her friends were almost all members of the athletic teams of the school. Because of her testimony the top athletes in this university were introduced to the ongoing religious renewal through the prayer groups.

There are many prayer groups in action mornings, afternoons, and evenings. There are prayer groups in the homes, at the universities, in plants, offices, and in state and federal buildings. The morning and afternoon sessions in the homes naturally gather mostly women. The men, in most cases, are at work at that time. Instead, the men may have morning prayer meetings at work or prayer meetings at lunch in a nearby cafeteria. In the evenings in prayer meetings at different homes the men also participate. On weekends "family prayer meetings" are held. In these meetings one sees grandmothers and grandfathers, as well as small babies, and all ages between.

In the prayer groups no denominational borderlines exist. These people meet together joined by what they have in common, unconcerned about differences of belief. Of course, they know each other's church preferences and dogmatical differences, but now they meet only as fellow Christians to share one another's testimonies of rejoicing and religious needs. Because of this, one may see in a single group Baptists, Lutherans, Methodists, Episcopalians, Presbyterians, Seventh Day Adventists, Catholics, and others.

Ministers and priests also come to these meetings, not as "clergy," but as participants. Because they usually have the most knowledge of the Bible, they can answer some of the more difficult questions which may come up. But, besides that, they are just ordinary participants, which means that they sometimes "only" sit and listen. They don't seem to see the prayer groups as a "threat" to the regular programs of their churches, but as a blessed amplification. "My people attending interdenominational prayer meetings always become better members of the church," one minister said.

"BEAR YE ONE ANOTHER'S BURDENS. . . ."

To describe in words the dynamic of a prayer gathering is impossible, for one is not like the other. It seems, however, as if every time the meeting starts with singing. One sings new and old earnest, devoted songs and hymns, often with the words taken directly from the Holy Scriptures. People sing with such a warmth and expectation that while singing they "feel" the presence of the Lord, which leads to thankfulness and faith. One dares come forth with one's prayer requests—almost everybody mentions something, and not always about themselves! Certainly they want prayers for their children, their wives, or husbands; but they also ask for prayers to be offered for their neighbors, for missionaries, for the president, for the government. The participants generally sit in a circle, and sometimes when they pray, they hold hands to really manifest the oneness in the prayers and the willingness to help one another in prayer. A rule from the Bible is visibly obeyed: "Bear ye one another's burdens and thus fulfill the law of Christ" (Gal. 6:2).

Sometimes they feel so intensely for one prayer request that they may choose to pray for only that. Sometimes they even fast! One really takes in another's problems and helps the other in prayer. A great confidence in each other is apparent as they open up their inner needs in a Christian fellowship beyond all borderlines. "It is like this," somebody said once, "when one comes to the Lord and asks for forgiveness, the Lord takes everything and sinks it into the bottom of the sea. Then he puts up a sign which reads, 'No fishing.' " When they meet later and talk, they talk about "how good God is," about "God's interference," and about "answers to prayers."

Sometimes there is someone, and sometimes there are many, who are seeking God's help and strength for some waiting task. Then the others gather around the ones who have asked for help and, with laying on of hands, again the communion is manifested in prayers for each other. The ones who were most eager to pray for others do not hesitate later on to seek help in prayer for some specific personal need. A strong faith in God and what He can do is demonstrated. The gifts of the Spirit are practiced. Speaking words of wisdom and counseling is a natural part of the atmosphere of being surrendered to the Lord. This may be directed to one person or to all in the group. All of this is genuine and spontaneous, and one feels at home in this little group and able to relax.

One of the participants in a prayer group, a lady in her forties, for a long time had prayed for a male relative of hers of the same age. This man was hospitalized in paralysis because of damage to the brain. The disease had caused the family deep sorrow, and the prognosis of the disease was grave. During one prayer meeting words of consolation were spoken to the woman by one of the ladies who said to her that through the Holy Spirit she should be able to feel calm and confident, because she was to be used as God's instrument to help and counsel sick people. These words helped her, and after the prayer meeting she went to the hospital where her relative was hospitalized. His condition had become increasingly worse, and during the last two months he had not been able to move his arms and hands. In humble faith the lady did according to the Scriptures and laid her hands on the sick man and said,

"Jesus Christ, you are the same yesterday, today, and forever. You have all power. May your perfect will be done, now!" During this prayer the man grasped her hand!! She could not believe her eyes. Had *she* lifted *his* hand or had *he himself* really lifted it? She was not quite sure, but soon she was because after this first beginning the man's range of movements increased, not only in the arm, but also in general day by day until he, some time later, was so rehabilitated and strong that he even went back to work!

PRAYERS FOR SISTER-IN-LAW

A lady from a prayer group tells us, "We had upon several occasions prayed for a sister-in-law of one of the participants in the group. About two years earlier this sister-in-law had fallen ill in deep depressions which had reached their peak when her teen-aged daughter left home. All this time the poor sister-in-law had been unable to do anything. For hours she just sat on a chair and looked apathetically out through a window. She did not look after her house or even take care of herself—not combing her hair or taking a shower. Now, our friend from the prayer group felt led to earnestly pray for her sister-in-law. She believed absolutely that this sister-in-law would be healed. Three of her friends volunteered to specifically help in her prayers, and thus during one week these four ladies met every morning for special prayers. One morning the other ladies heard one of them pray, "Lord, let our sister go to the hairdresser to your glory, let her put on her make-up to your glory! Soon!"

Something remarkable happened—the sister-in-law started from that day on to take care of herself, the house, and everything else. She had come to life again! Soon she was able to attend to her duties as a mother and wife one hundred percent, calm and as happy as ever before. "The situation with our daughter is unchanged," she says, "but we know that God is going to intercede soon and bring the whole family together again!"

PRAYERS FOR FINANCIAL PROBLEMS

In another testimony from a prayer group meeting, a young housewife tells this story: "I was here for the first time a week ago, and I asked for your prayers. I am sure you remember how I embarrassed myself and cried and told you about our financial problems and about a great many other problems. Everything seemed so hopeless. I did not see any way out. There were many bills to be paid, and we did not have any money. You prayed together with me, and you looked up Bible passages, showing that the Lord not only fills out spiritual needs, but also our everyday requirements. You did not know me. You just counseled me and showed me love anyway by helping me to turn everything over to the Lord. I am sure you do not recognize me now—I am so happy—and thankful to God! What happened was that my father and mother-in-law—they live here in this city too—came over to our place the other day. They had not been visiting for quite some time. When they left, they gave us an envelope with money in it! Just enough to pay all the bills!! Never before have they given us money, and we are sure that they did not have the slightest idea what our situation was at the time!"

PRAYER GROUPS HAVE
NO ETHNIC BOUNDARIES

A physician's wife was, about a year ago, the one about whom everybody in the town talked. . . . She had spoken in tongues—not publicly, but she did it in her prayers by herself. When she related what had happened, she said she had just been praying by herself in her room, when suddenly she used another language than her own. She, as well as her husband and children, is Episcopalian. The

41

doctor is one of the leaders of the church and also a choir member. The doctor's wife is very active in the different ladies' activities in the church. After her charismatic experience she continued her services to the church as usual. She also started a prayer group in her home. Prayer meetings were something new for the ladies in her circle of acquaintances. But they saw that something great had happened to their best friend. She had always been a calm, humble, and happy type of person. Now she became even calmer and more humble, and at the same time, more open and happier. She often told her friends about her experience of the Holy Spirit and how that had changed her devotional life and refined her relationship to her family and husband. Everyday everything was much deeper and more meaningful. God was in everything day by day. More and more of her "upper class ladies" in the town where she lives came to the prayer meetings. They became so fascinated by God's presence in people's lives that they also started to attend other prayer meetings. In these meetings they met people from other social strata as well. One by one they started to live new lives through the baptism of the Holy Spirit.

The doctor's wife was the chairlady for the women's club of her church. "Why don't I ask them all to come to my house for tea next time? Maybe God in that way will make the meeting something extra," she thought to herself one day. What she had in mind was to invite both the ladies from the women's club and the ladies from the prayer group at the same time. One thing she knew for sure—the Lord would send the right people for the program. Time after time lately she had experienced just that! The right persons had arrived for the right circumstances. And God can use anyone open to His calling!!

The morning of the day when the tea was going to take place, one of her new friends called on the phone and said,

"I feel led to come to your house today and bring four ladies from our prayer group. They have some wonderful testimonies to share, and I will bring the guitar and lead the singing."

At the teaparty all the ladies joined to sing, among others, the Jesus People's "Hallelujah Song." Everyone sang. The Spirit of the Lord was present. "We all felt how the presence of God lifted us all to His reality," one of the participants told us later. The prayer meeting which followed formed a natural part of the program. A lady who helped with preparing the food for the party also was invited to participate. She was a refined, beautiful lady with copper-toned skin and dark, gentle eyes—eyes which always smiled, it seemed. The kitchen was filled with the dishes used at the party, but the dishwashing had to wait. This black lady became the white ladies' "sister," both inside the prayer group circle and also outside. When she came into the prayer meeting, some of the ladies hugged her; and when God later in the meeting talked through a prophetic message directly to her, all cried with happiness and thankfulness for the opportunity to experience again a glimpse of heaven already on earth and for a self-explanatory sisterhood reaching beyond all boundaries, including man-made racial barriers.

In the kitchen one noticed that the doctor had stood and opened the refrigerator to look for something to eat for lunch. His morning operations were successfully performed. He was smiling in spite of the fact that no lunch table was set yet and no luncheon served, for here in his house people had met the Lord in the middle of the day!

HOUSEWIFE—HIPPIE

Many more examples could be related. Here is just one more. A young housewife has been in a charismatic group for three years. She is a member of a downtown

Presbyterian church. "Before I came to the Lord," she says, "I was a housewife addict. I took pills morning, afternoon, and night. I drank until I became intoxicated at parties, and my husband often had to carry me to our car. I was known for my filthy jokes." Now she is saved and filled with the Holy Spirit and a hard, eager worker in the kingdom of the Lord.

One day she was in charge of the program of the women's organization of her church. The meeting takes place in a home, and everything is precise and sophisticated. Most of the participants are considered leading ladies in this city. To the meeting today she has invited a young student—a girl who had become a Christian about a year earlier. The girl had been deeply involved in narcotics. At a pop festival she had met a boy whom she had married after only two weeks. Neither of them worked. Instead, they spent their time smoking marijuana and listening to music. After one year of big difficulties they were divorced. In the meantime a little baby girl had been born, and the student was now left alone with her small baby. Now, at this ladies meeting, she gave her testimony of how God had saved her, set her free from her drug dependence, given her happiness and harmony, and how she had gone back to school. All the ladies were moved by the testimony, and afterwards were invited to a charismatic prayer meeting. During this meeting, a physician's wife asked the participants to pray for her and her sister who had alcoholic problems. Many spoke silently in tongues and prayed quietly. The physician's wife, who had never before seen or heard anything like it, was so moved and blessed that she immediately told her friends about it and a new prayer group started. Well, between fifteen and twenty ladies in that prayer group are now Spirit-filled.

The prayer groups revival increases day by day. This is what the participants in a prayer group presented at the beginning of this chapter also realize. Their prayer meeting for today has just ended. People hug each other and start to get their Bibles, bags, and coats together. One of the ladies looks at her watch more as a reflex than a necessity. "Is this really possible—we have been here more than three hours!" she says. "Remarkable. Three hours just disappeared in an intense reality."

No wonder that these people, immensely strengthened and spiritually renewed, went back to the chores of a time-scheduled day beautified through the reality of God's very presence.

CHAPTER 5

Sunday

The cars are rolling slowly as they turn through the gates and up the gravel roads toward the Chapel. There are no signs or posters at the gates or outside the building to indicate what kind of a place we are approaching.

Many cars are already parked everywhere underneath the century-old oak trees in the park-like lawn. From this we understand that many worshippers have already arrived almost an hour before the service is scheduled to start.

Judging by the cars a rather "mixed" group has come to this, God's place, today. We find small cars and trucks, late models of sport cars, and also, big expensive new cars parked side by side with five- or ten-year-old ones.

Many, including the luxury car owners, have glued bumper stickers on their cars. The signs read, for instance, like these: "One Way," "Jesus Loves You," "Guess Who's Coming Again," "I Am, You Are, HE IS," "Our God Is Not Dead, Sorry about Yours," "Tell It Like It Is: John 3:16."

WHAT IS THE SECRET?

The prayer meetings and Bible studies we have described here have never been advertised on TV, in the newspapers, or on posters. People have come and are coming anyway.

The home in the oak park is literally packed this Sunday morning—more than 300! During the long time we have been attending the Chapel, it has always been filled. Besides that, the crowds were always renewed. Every time we saw new faces, visitors from other cities! How is it possible to gather so many people without advertising in the news media? How did the people know about it? What is the secret of the epidemic increase in the charismatic movement? How does a movement of this kind come about? How are most people recruited for new ideas? Through the enthusiasm of individuals: Every day! At work! At home! Everywhere! Always! Among relatives, friends, and people everyplace!

The success depends on sincere personal contacts between people. It is through "the mouth-to-mouth method" that new participants are recruited to the prayer groups. And in prayer groups in this city everybody talks about what is happening in other prayer groups such as the one in the Chapel. This is the way that people come to know about the meetings at the Chapel. One receives a blessing and tells his friends about it. People call each other and people talk about it when they meet socially. The word goes around from person to person. A chain reaction develops! The blessings are shared! It is this which is the secret of public relations, and it is this which makes them so effective!

Through these means the Chapel has been filled this Sunday morning as it has been Sunday after Sunday since its inception. There is a hum of expectation at least half an hour ahead of the time when the meeting is scheduled to start. People come smiling up to one another, hug each other, or shake hands. One nods at friends sitting a little bit away or talks to the neighbor on the next chair. It is like one big family.

THE SINGING

Both the piano player and the organist are already in

place. The organist is Brother Bill's wife. She is also of Indian heritage—of the Osage tribe. She looks as if she had just walked out of a picturebook—she is so nice and beautiful! In her professional life she is a schoolteacher.

The pianist used to have his own group when he worked in show business. Both are playing their instruments at the same time. They play well-known and loved hymns, and people all over the building sing or hum to the music. Then someone starts to clap hands, and others do the same. One sings louder and louder, and soon all have joined in singing:

> Would you be free from the burden of sin?
> There's pow'r in the blood, pow'r in the blood:
> Would you o'er evil a victory win?
> There's wonderful pow'r in the blood.
>
> There is pow'r, pow'r, Wonder-working pow'r
> In the blood of the Lamb;
> There is pow'r, pow'r, Wonder-working pow'r
> In the precious blood of the Lamb.

Just at eleven o'clock a man comes up to the front of the people, says a cheery good morning, and starts leading the singing of the song which the people have already started, with great fervor and warmth. One understands from the relaxed way of conducting the singing that he is used to standing in front of an audience. As a matter of fact, he has been a song leader for many years and has heard and seen different groups of people sing. But never before did he find an audience giving such a response, and never before did he see such spontaneity and reality, as among these people. No wonder that this place is radiating happiness. The entire congregation now sings, so blessed and moved by the wonder of the songs that every corner of the big house is filled with the Glory of God.

The singing forms an important part of the service. It is not any particular kind of singing; it is not there only to fill a spot in the program. It is not always the many and long stanzas of a hymn. No, often one sings the same choruses over and over again—until it feels as if it is a part of one's inner world. One sings lively songs, such as "Victory in Jesus" and "There is power, power, wonder-working power." In these songs the secrets of a victorious life are proclaimed. The songs about victory are inter-changed with songs of a more silent and devotional nature, such as "Oh, how I love Jesus," "His Name is Wonderful," and "Thank you, Lord for saving my soul." Very often one sings the prayer song—"Fill my cup, Lord."

Every church seems to have a choir, but in the Chapel there is no separate choir. The singing congregation as a whole is the choir, and in this choir there are many good singers and soloists. Spontaneously, these singers harmonize. No choir ever sounds more beautiful than the singing in unison of anointed people—such as in the Chapel!

This does not mean that professional singers or singing groups present are excluded from the blessings of serving with their talents. On the contrary! Almost every time some soloist or singing group participates. An obvious humble-ness is present among the professional singers when they come to the Chapel. Here, more than anyplace else, they come to realize that without the anointing of the Holy Spirit their singing would be of no meaning, so they feel it important that the Holy Spirit leads them in the choice of their songs. One prays to be a blessing to at least someone. This humbleness has made many singers to be God's instrument in a special way at the Chapel.

This Sunday a singer has been asked to sing the song, "How Great Thou Art." This Swedish song has been a blessing to literally millions of people. Before the singing the soloist says that she sang the same song in a service in another place a couple of weeks earlier. She had been prepared to sing another song when God told her to first sing one verse of "How Great Thou Art," and to sing it in Swedish. After the service a lady radiating happiness and joy rushed forward to hug the singer. The lady said that only about a month ago she had been baptized in the Holy Spirit. Now she had asked the Lord for His special blessing and keeping when trying to serve Him in a new way. She was born in Sweden, and during twenty-two years away from her home country this was the first time she had heard someone singing in Swedish! She would never have dreamed that God's promises—to be with us always in a personal way—should be confirmed to her in Swedish!

After the singing all join in prayers for some persons who had requested special prayers. All take their neighbors' hands as a sign of oneness and trust in God for whom nothing is impossible. It is moving to see all the families standing together holding hands as they pray—father, mother, teenagers, little sisters and brothers. Before "the Throne of Grace" the kinship increases to its peak. As a matter of fact, there are many children in the Chapel. They all seem to be alert and interested. Some have even placed themselves on the floor at the front of the room to be able to see and hear better. As much as is possible this meeting is exactly like the one in the marketplace in the Swedish town between the mountains!

"SINGING IN THE SPIRIT"

The service proceeds in a relaxed atmosphere without ceremonies and without a program in which every detail is planned ahead. More singing! When a few rather simple-to-learn choruses have been sung quietly and repeatedly, one hears a young man with a clear, distinct voice start singing a mass—like a priest—with liturgical intonation. The words in the mass are filled with consolation and edification and are very skillfully formed. They sound like

50

poetry and are about the Almighty's love and solicitude toward people, and how God sees and knows all our needs, and how he really is present in everything that happens. Everything becomes quiet and calm in the Chapel, for al understand that a miracle is taking place! All know that the young man who is now singing the mass is doing it "in the Spirit." They know that neither he nor any other person would ever be able to form such beautiful words by himself. Futhermore, they know that the boy does not have a singing voice of his own!

All experience this message as directly from the Lord.

The mass is followed by quiet prayers and the "Hallelujah Song" originated among the Jesus people.

THE SERMON

Now one sees Brother Bill proceed to the rostrum. All had, one after another, by and by, stood up during the Hallelujah Song. Standing, everybody now joins in the reading in unison from the Scriptures the Words which form the basis for the sermon today.

"And Jesus went out, and his disciples, into the towns of Caesarea Philippi; and on the way he asked his disciples, saying unto them, Who do men say that I am? And they answered, John the Baptist; but some say Elijah; and others, One of the prophets" (Mark 8:27-28).

Brother Bill talks about the importance of not jumping to conclusions and urges the congregation to always wait with their judgments. "We are often too fast with our judgments about people," he says. "After our first contact with a person we are all ready to give our evaluation for or against a person. If we just wait a little bit, we are saved the humiliation of later being forced to withdraw hasty conclusions. It is always difficult to admit a mistake.

"As we can see from the Scripture we just read, Jesus also met wrong judgments and conclusions," Brother Bill

51

continues. "That happened on several occasions. Remember, for instance, what happened, when they came to Jesus and told Him that Lazarus was sick? Jesus did not immediately go to see Lazarus. First, a couple of days passed, then Jesus started towards Bethany. When He arrived, Lazarus was dead. It is certain that some people at once were ready to say: 'Look there, Jesus did not care about His old friend Lazarus. Had he done so he would, of course, have started on His way immediately.' Had they waited with their judgments a little while they would, as their first words in this matter, have been able to testify to the miracle that Jesus brought Lazarus back from the dead."

Brother Bill speaks at a rather quick tempo, his voice is clear, distinct, and eager. The message is on a level which everybody understands. It is simple without being poor. It is teaching at the same time as it is reawakening. Brother Bill often takes his examples from personal experiences to be able to clarify and point to what he wants to get across. "We are often ready to condemn what other people do because we are not ourselves interested in what they are doing. I remember from my time as a student at the seminary how a group of us boys liked to exercise and keep in good physical condition through football. We took advantage of our free time exercising! There were also a couple of boys who were not at all interested in football and constantly told us that we would probably be lost forever because of playing football. But our classmates were interested in hunting and fishing. They would be away for a couple of days in total seclusion where nobody could reach them. There is nothing wrong with total relaxation sometimes. But at the seminary it would have been ideal if everybody had been as easy to reach as we were. People in need of counseling often came to the seminary for spiritual help. We football players were always on hand because the football field was part of our campus, and we interrupted our play to speak to these people and to pray with them. When we pointed this out to our friends, they realized that they had been unwise when they had criticized us. Therefore, wait with your judgment. It belongs to the Lord. Amen."

WINDS OF LOVE AROUND HIS TABLE

The sermon is over, and Brother Bill leads the congregation to sing a chorus. During the singing the preparation for the Holy Communion takes place. There is communion every Sunday at the Chapel. Men of different ages—young men with long hair, older men with short hair—come forward to help serve the emblems. The grape juice is served in small individual glass cups. Every participant holds the bread and the juice until all are served. Brother Richard reads the well-known Bible verses about how Holy Communion was ordained by Jesus:

For I have received of the Lord that which also I delivered unto you, that the Lord Jesus, the same night in which he was betrayed, took bread; And when he had given thanks, he broke it, and said, Take, eat, this is my body, which is broken for you: this do in remembrance of me. After the same manner also he took the cup, when he had supped, saying, This cup is the new testament in my blood: this do as often as ye drink it in remembrance of me (I Cor. 11:23-25).

After the reading he prays, moved by the occasion. All take the bread at the same time and, afterwards, the juice. An atmosphere of closeness and kinship fills the house. Everywhere people express in different ways their thankfulness for the grace of God represented through the sacraments. Some lift their hands. Others whisper, "Thank you, Lord." Others cry softly. One stops for a moment in silence before God. The silence lifts the soul! Fruitful ideas for tomorrow are born!

SHAKE HANDS WITH NINETY-NINE

The service is coming toward its end. No collection of money has taken place during the service! This is never done in the Chapel. There are no fervent talks asking you to give money. Everyone who feels called to give money may do so. And they do! Up until today all expenses have been abundantly met!

Brother Bill adds as a final remark that love for our neighbors is significant in every Christian life and reads from I John 3:14: "We know that we have passed from death unto life, because we love the brethren. He that loveth not his brother abideth in death."

"Before you leave this place, greet as many people as possible. At least ninety-nine! Take time for this and tell them that Jesus loves them and you love them." While singing "We'll Give the Glory to Jesus," people start following Brother Bills' advice to greet as many persons as possible.

If you are not used to it, you may feel a little bit numb afterwards because of all the hugs, handshakes, and kisses. But the warmth and love in these greetings is impossible to deny—it is like a shower. We do not count the number of persons we meet nor the number of "Jesus loves you" and "God Bless You's" we receive, but they are certainly not few!

Everywhere one sees happy, radiant faces, faces expressing love, love, and more love. "By this shall all men know that ye are my disciples, if ye love one another" (John 13:35).

CHAPTER 6

Open House for Bible Studies

And daily in the temple, and in every house, they ceased not to teach and preach Jesus Christ
(Acts 5:42).

It is 10 o'clock in the morning of a brilliant, crystal clear, winter day, when people meet for a Bible study in a home a couple of miles out from the downtown area of a typical American metropolitan area. The lady of the house, a Presbyterian, has found a new meaning in her life through the charismatic renewal. She is now standing at the doorway of her beautiful house greeting people as they come. The warmth in her eyes and handshake is impossible for anybody to miss. She invites us into a large room tastefully decorated. A sofa and a couple of matching chairs of different types have been placed to form a circle. Everybody this way gets closer to each other. Soon about 10 ladies between the ages of twenty and sixty have come. Brother Bill has been asked to lead the Bible study. He has come and so have a couple of other men.

Most of the Bible study participants have interesting testimonies to share about how the charismatic renewal changed their lives. A young housewife is relating first to some of the ladies closest to her, then to all, how she earlier always was afraid of everything. Among other things, she was afraid of flying. She became "hysterical" when she went up in an airplane. Fear of many things really terrorized her. With the charismatic renewal, however, a marked change within her took place. This came to a test sometime later when she had to travel by air on a long tour. She was not at all afraid anymore! Her phobia had disappeared! She even felt the flight exciting!

"SOME TO TEACHERS"

At her side a dark-haired lady about 30 years old with lively dark brown eyes is sitting. Her entire beautiful face is filled with inner radiation. She comes regularly to these Bible studies. They totally fascinate her. But not only that, her input at these Bible studies is very meaningful.

About 10 years ago she graduated from a teachers' college with much knowledge of the teaching profession. When the charismatic renewal reached her, her knowledge acquired a new light. She was engaged in Bible study groups and was able to help many through her deep insight as well as her schooling and teaching talents. Her spirit-filled personality radiated love and compassion! Everything testified to charisma—God's gifts in function!

JEWS HEAR SPEAKING IN
TONGUES IN HEBREW

To the Bible study today somebody has brought a Jewish couple. They have veritably experienced almost too much lately. They had come to the Chapel for the first time just a few weeks earlier. One had noticed them from the very first minute they arrived, mainly because of the man's enormous hair—among the bushiest we had ever seen.

Both were dressed in jeans and shirts hanging out. At her second visit to the Chapel one Tuesday evening the woman had requested prayers because of bad health. Her physicians had said that the disease she had no longer could be controlled through medication, and all were troubled when considering the outcome. The man had also come forward for counseling and prayers. When they were praying they heard Brother Bill talk to them in Hebrew! It was about God's love and that God cared about them and that God was going to heal the woman's disease. Neither of the two knew that Brother Bill did not speak Hebrew. He had spoken in tongues in their language! The Jewish man had been a teacher of Hebrew in Israel for many years!

What took place in those minutes cannot be explained, they told us afterwards. They had not only felt an inner spiritual lift, but the woman also had felt that something happened to her health. And she was not wrong! From that day her health returned slowly but positively.

The first evening, when they came home from the Chapel, they burned their books on Transcendental Meditation, which especially the woman had studied earlier and from which she had given courses. All night, almost into the sunrise, they studied a New Testament which had been placed in their hands. As Jews, they had up until that time read only the Old Testament! When they now read through the New Testament, they clearly saw Jesus as their Messiah. Jesus became the total answer for them —historically, philosophically, and religiously. They wanted to follow him in all. They believed his words about baptism and the promise of the Holy Spirit. They wanted to know more about this and, therefore, contacted Christian brothers and sisters for further Bible studies.

The following Sunday they were baptized, and following the baptismal ceremony they were filled with the Holy Spirit. New persons to both spirit, soul, and body within a week! No wonder that they look happy sitting on the sofa next to each other. What was the secret to this series of unexpected happenings in their lives? "We had always said to each other that if we saw the love which Jesus told about functioning among Christians, then we would immediately accept Him. When we came and saw and experienced the love among these Christians, we believed and surrendered our lives to Jesus Christ. We did not have the slightest idea that this should give us so very many blessings."

At the left side of the couple, a group of ladies are sitting. Now before the Bible study has started they chat livelily, gesticulate, and laugh heartily. A "praise the Lord" is heard in the middle of all this. So obviously they talk about an interference of some kind through the Lord.

Someone starts to sing and others join in. One sings reverently directly from the Bible: "I will lift up my hands in thy name" (Psalms: 63:46).

Quite a few do exactly what they sing: they lift their hands in thanksgiving to the Lord for his grace, which is better than everything in life. The lifting of the hands seems natural and genuine and not stereotyped. It is like when one is moving his hands while talking to someone. In this case the movements of arms and hands in some way free a person for a new dimension and closeness in his experience of God. God has become real to them even on weekdays, and they are permitted to talk to Him as they are—with gestures and all.

Now everybody quiets down and is waiting in expectation for the Bible study to start. They sit down and take their Bibles. It is obvious that the interest is great. The subject today is "The Holy Spirit." All are listening, and an audible sound from the pages of the Bibles fills the room as many hands eagerly try to find the presented passages in the Scriptures. They also take notes and ask questions whenever there is something they cannot understand. The participants are always eager to learn and alert. In a clear way Brother Bill has listed the main points and supporting Bible verses on posters, which he holds up so everyone sees. The tempo is rather quick and purposeful. There are many verses of Scripture they are able to cover during this very well-planned and prepared lecture.

When the Bible study is over this time and some questions have been answered, the meeting ends by all standing up in a circle holding hands and praying. "A feeling impossible to describe!" one of the lady participants told us a couple of days later. "When I came back to the chores of every day, the assurance followed me that I again by Grace had experienced something great."

ONE WEEK LATER

One week has gone. The same home. The same weekday and the same time of the day: It is winter weather. While the snow quietly falls, one by one of the ones who were here a week ago are coming. Almost all of them have come back today plus quite a few others. So today more than 20 persons are present.

Among the newcomers is a housewife about 30 years old. She is a Southern Baptist. About a year ago she experienced a religious renewal through the baptism in the Holy Spirit. She now gives her testimony: "Some friends who had been filled with the Holy Spirit told me about it. During a long time I had been praying to God to give me more power in my Christian life and started to pray that Jesus might fill me with the Spirit. My prayers were answered. But not in the dramatic way which I had anticipated. When I received the baptism in the Holy Spirit it came very naturally and quietly. I did not feel any increased lift of my mood level. I was already happy and thankful to the Lord. The reason for this was that my husband had come back to the Lord two weeks earlier. He had been backsliding for three years! Both of us were very happy. Now we were praying together about the Holy Spirit. As we were praying, both of us started in tongues —I believe at the same time! We experienced this as beautiful and real and healthy. The language of the angels just poured out from the inside like a warm wind. We thanked the Lord for His great love to us in the prayer service in which this happened. But in the middle of the service, I started to be doubtful about what I had just experienced. Had I really been filled with the Spirit? Was this real? Could the baptism in the Holy Spirit be that simple? During an entire week I had these doubts. But after having reasoned with myself quoting verses from the Scriptures, and after having talked it over with others, who had had similar experiences, I was sure that what had happened to me was the baptism in the Holy Spirit."

To the Bible study today the former dancer has also come. We know her from before. An interesting episode, which was very important for her coming to the Lord, had happened some years ago. She was sitting with her parents in a restaurant, and they were talking in their native language. A woman missionary, home on furlough, this day also "happened" to have lunch at the same place, and heard this other company speaking a foreign language. When she took the opportunity to ask them about their home country, what she really wanted was to talk to them about the Lord. They talked together for a while. The missionary soon after this incident went to her field. Out there she felt led to pray especially for the beautiful young dancer whom she had met in a restaurant on the other side of the world. This woman even became the constant subject of her prayers!

When the missionary came home on furlough the next time, she was called to speak in one of the churches in the same city where she had met the young artist the last time she was home. Whom do you think she saw in the congregation? The woman from the restaurant! A crisis in her life had led her to God. Just as the missionary once many months ago had grasped an opportunity to testify about the Lord, so the dancer now always testifies about her Master. She is a wonderful burning witness for the Lord—a frank winner of souls!

Some others have interesting happenings to tell testifying to God's presence in big and small events in their personal lives day by day. Once again they sing a song, and the Bible study continues where they stopped last week. The intensive, well-disciplined lecture proceeds.

When the Bible study is over for the day, it is followed by a time of prayer. One of the ladies, here for her first time, asks for special prayers. She is only visiting this city and she does not know anyone present, but she feels that these people have something which she does not have. With tears in her eyes she prays to the Lord to give her the fullness of His Spirit. The others help her in prayer, and have other prayer requests. Some want help in prayers for their children; others for their husbands or wives. They all take one another's hands and pray, urgently and personally. The sense of togetherness is stong and real.

When the prayer time is over, they all hug each other or wave to each other from a distance. It looks as if everybody tries to reach everyone else who has been present with a personal word or touch. Some travel straight home; others go out for lunch together or go to the health club for their daily exercise program and for the many opportunities to give their testimonies. But they have one thing in common—they all look energetic and strengthened.

CHAPTER 7

A Continuous Bible Study in a Home

Some examples of home Bible studies and questions which usually are asked in connection with these are compiled in this chapter.

The following is from a Bible study group which meets one morning a week. Every time they continue where they stopped the week before. This continuous Bible study deals with the Holy Spirit, the Baptism of the Holy Spirit, and the Gifts of the Spirit. For the participants such topics are completely relevant. In a very real way the religious experience, which the Bible calls the Baptism in the Holy Spirit, has radically and deeply changed their whole persons and whole lives. They know how this experience has changed them inside and out, how this change was the beginning of great blessings, and how they afterwards day by day have seen more and more of the gifts of the Spirit in function. To them one consequently talks about real things.

"Today we start with the 'personal qualities' of the Holy Spirit," the Bible study leader, Brother Bill, says. "The Holy Spirit has:

Mind—

> And he that searcheth the hearts knoweth what is the mind of the Spirit, because he maketh intercession for the saints according to the will of God (ROMANS 8:27).

Will—

But all these worketh that one and the selfsame Spirit, dividing to every man severally as he will

(1 CORINTHIANS 12:11).

Feeling—

And grieve not the holy Spirit of God, whereby ye are sealed unto the day of redemption

(EPHESIANS 4:30).

"The holy spirit also performs certain activities, namely:

Reveals—

For the prophecy came not in old time by the will of man: but holy men of God spake as they were moved by the Holy Ghost (2 PETER 1:21).

Teaches—

But the Comforter, which is the Holy Ghost, whom the Father will send in my name, he shall teach you all things, and bring all things to your remembrance, whatsoever I have said unto you

(JOHN 14:26).

Witnesses—

The Spirit himself beareth witness with our spirit, that we are the children of God (ROMANS 8:16).

Intercedes—

Likewise the Spirit also helpeth our infirmities: for we know not what we should pray for as we ought: but the Spirit himself maketh intercession for us with groanings which cannot be uttered

(ROMANS 8:26).

Speaks—

>He that hath an ear, let him hear what the Spirit saith unto the churches (REVELATION 2: 7a).

Commands—

>Now when they had gone throughout Phrygia and the region of Galatia and were forbidden of the Holy Ghost to preach the word in Asia, After they were come to Mysia, they assayed to go into Bithynia: but the Spirit suffered them not
>
>(ACTS 16:6, 7).

Testifies—

>But when the Comforter is come, whom I will send unto you from the Father, even the Spirit of truth, which proceedeth from the Father, he shall testify of me (JOHN 15:26).

"The Holy Spirit may be:

Grieved—

>And grieve not the holy Spirit of God
>
>(EPHESIANS 4:30).

Lied to—

>But Peter said, Ananias, why hath Satan filled thine heart to lie to the Holy Ghost, and to keep back part of the price of the land? (ACTS 5:3).

Blasphemed—

>Wherefore I say unto you, All manner of sin and blasphemy shall be forgiven unto men: but the blasphemy against the Holy Ghost shall not be forgiven unto men (MATTHEW 12:31).

The teaching is skillfully concentrated. The essential

points are illustrated with examples from personal experiences.

"The Bible has many different names on the Holy Ghost," Brother Bill continues, and refers to Scriptural passage after Scriptural passage.

"The Holy Spirit is called:

The Spirit of God—
Know ye not that ye are the temple of God and that the Spirit of God dwelleth in you?
(1 CORINTHIANS 3:16).

The Spirit of Jesus Christ—
For I know that this shall turn to my salvation through your prayer, and the supply of the Spirit of Jesus Christ (PHIL. 1:19).

The Comforter—
But the Comforter, which is the Holy Ghost, whom the Father will send in my name
(JOHN 14:26a).

The Spirit of Truth—
Even the Spirit of truth; whom the world cannot receive, because it seeth him not, neither knoweth him (JOHN 14:17a).

The Spirit of Grace—
Of how much sorer punishment, suppose ye, shall he be thought worthy, who hath trodden under foot the Son of God, and hath counted the blood of the covenant, wherewith he was sanctified, an unholy thing, and hath done despite unto the Spirit of grace? (HEBREWS 10:29).

The Spirit of Life—

65

> For the law of the Spirit of life in Christ Jesus
> hath made me free from the law of sin and death
> (ROMANS 8:2).

The Spirit of Adoption—

> For ye have not received the spirit of bondage
> again to fear; but ye have received the Spirit of
> adoption, whereby we cry, Abba, Father
> (ROMANS 8:15).

"The Holy Spirit is also mentioned under different symbols, such as:

Fire—

> He shall baptize you with the Holy Ghost, and
> with fire (MATTHEW 3:11b).

Wind—

> And suddenly there came a sound from heaven
> as of a rushing mighty wind and it filled all the
> house where they were sitting (ACTS 2:2).

Water—

> He that believeth on me, as the scripture hath
> said, out of his belly shall flow rivers of living
> water. But this spake he of the Spirit, which they
> that believe on him should receive
> (JOHN 7:38, 39a).

Seal—

> in whom also after that ye believed, ye were sealed
> with the holy Spirit of promise
> (EPHESIANS 1:13b).

Dove—

> And Jesus, when he was baptized, went up

> straightway out of the water: and, lo, the heavens were opened unto him, and he saw the Spirit of God descending like a dove, and lighting upon him (MATTHEW 3:16).

So fast the time has gone. It's already after the time this Bible study usually stops, so after a short prayer everyone has to hurry home today.

One week has passed and it is time to meet again. They enjoy and share happiness and sorrows before it is time to start the Bible study. Soon it is silent, and everyone looks full of expectation at the Bible study leader, Brother Bill, who says, "Today we'll continue talking about the Holy Spirit and above all about the gifts of the Spirit. Let's all read from 1 Corinthians 12:8-11."

They read together:

"For to one is given by the Spirit the word of wisdom; to another the word of knowledge by the same Spirit; to another faith by the same Spirit; to another the gifts of healing by the same Spirit; to another the working of miracles; to another prophecy; to another discerning of spirits; to another divers kinds of tongues; to another the interpretation of tongues. But all these worketh that one and the selfsame Spirit, dividing to every man severally as he will."

"God has given the gifts to be used in the church," he continues. "The gifts are not only for preachers or certain selected people, but for every believer.

> And these signs shall follow them that believe; In my name shall they cast out devils; they shall speak with new tongues; They shall take up serpents; and if they drink any deadly thing, it shall not hurt them; they shall lay hands on the sick, and they shall recover (MARK 16:17, 18).

67

"The gifts of the Spirit are always supernatural. The gifts are supernatural, not we, even if we sometimes seem to think we are. We point at ourselves and say, 'I have that or that spiritual gift,' or 'The Lord speaks through me.' When I hear things like that I usually say that the Lord even can speak through a donkey, if he wishes. He spoke, for instance, through Balaam's donkey, according to Numbers 22:28-30:

> And the Lord opened the mouth of the ass, and she said unto Balaam, What have I done unto thee, that thou hast smitten me these three times? And Balaam said unto the ass, Because thou hast mocked me: I would there were a sword in mine hand, for now would I kill thee. And the ass said unto Balaam, Am not I thine ass, upon which thou hast ridden ever since I was thine unto this day? was I ever wont to do so unto thee? And he said, Nay.

"Sometimes we hear people say, referring to 1 Corinthians 13, that love is more important than the gifts of the Spirit. But if we study this passage a little closer, we clearly see that it is not an 'either-or,' but a 'both-and': *love and the gifts.* Love is one of the fruits of the Spirit. We can't have God's real love in us without having the Holy Spirit. The Bible urges us to seek both love and the gifts of the Spirit, 'Follow after charity, and desire spiritual gifts, but rather that ye may prophesy (1 CORINTHIANS 14:1).

"The spiritual gifts fall into three groups. The first three are gifts of revelation and have to do with *knowledge:*
1. To speak words of knowledge.
2. To speak words of wisdom.
3. Discerning of spirits.

"The next three are *vocal* gifts, which have to do with our speech. They are

1. Tongues.
2. Interpretation of tongues.
3. Prophecy.

"The remaining three are gifts of power, gifts on which we act:

1. The gift of faith.
2. The gifts of healing.
3. Works of miracles.

"Six of these nine gifts are functioning in the quiet. Because we can *hear* only three of them, some people believe that only these three are in function in the church today. But that is not the case. All the gifts are functioning through the Holy Spirit, and everyone can become an instrument for all the gifts. The gifts are not our own. God only uses us as channels for them!

"Let's talk a little more about the different gifts, and first about the gift to speak words of knowledge," the Bible study leader says. "First a few words about what this gift is *not*. It is *not* education or knowledge which one has assimilated, consequently not even knowledge about God or God's word, which anyone can learn through studying. It is not imagination or enlightened guesses and absolutely not witchcraft. The Bible warns very clearly and distinctly against witchcraft:

There shall not be found among you any one that maketh his son or his daughter to pass through the fire, or that useth divination, or an observer of times, or an enchanter, or a witch, Or a charmer, or a consulter with familiar spirits, or a wizard, or a necromancer. For all that do these things are an abomination unto the Lord: and because of these abominations the Lord thy God doth drive them out from before thee. Thou shalt be perfect with the Lord thy God. For these nations, which thou shalt possess, hearkened unto ob-

servers of times, and unto diviners: but as for thee, the Lord thy God hath not suffered thee so to do
                    (DEUTERONOMY 18:10-14).

And it came to pass, as we went to prayer, a certain damsel possessed with a spirit of divination met us, which brought her masters much gain by soothsaying:
The same followed Paul and us, and cried, saying, These men are the servants of the most high God, which shew unto us the way of salvation. And this did she many days. But Paul, being grieved, turned and said to the spirit, I command thee in the name of Jesus Christ to come out of her. And he came out the same hour (ACTS 16:16-18).

"Now, what is the gift of speaking the word of knowledge? It is a divine revelation of certain facts in a supernatural way through the Holy Spirit. This can happen through dreams, visions, revelations, or audible voice. The Bible gives many examples referring to God's giving knowledge to people and revealing secrets to them. Let us take a few examples from the Old as well as from the New Testament.

"When they were searching for Saul in order to crown him the king, they asked the Lord's advice where to find him. The Lord then answered, 'He hath hid himself among the stuff' (1 Samuel 10. 22b). They ran there and found him.

"When the Lord told Ananias to go and pray for Saul, he also told him where Saul was and what he was doing:

And the Lord said unto him, Arise, and go into the street which is called Straight, and inquire in the house of Judas for one called Saul, of Tarsus: for, behold, he prayeth (ACTS 9:11).

"The facts Jesus revealed for the woman at the well of Sychar, when He said that she had had five husbands, is another example of the same thing: 'For thou hast had five husbands; and he whom thou now hast is not thy husband: in that saidst thou truly' (John 4:18).

"Let us also take a couple of examples which have happened in our days. A pastor was on a tour driving his car. On the road he picked up two hitchhikers, and after awhile he asked them if they were saved. They said, "Yes." But he felt through the Holy Spirit that the hitchhikers were lying. And that was not all. The pastor felt convinced that the men had evil intentions—yes, that they were going to kill him! When the pastor and his two passengers came to a rest stop along the road, he therefore stopped and informed the two men that he had decided not to go any further that day.

"The men left, and the pastor soon saw them get a ride in another car. The following morning the pastor heard on the radio that someone had found a man who was seriously beaten by some hitchhikers. They had bound him to a tree, taken his car, and disappeared. Considerably later this man was found in a very bad condition. In spite of this he managed to give a good description of the hitchhikers. It corresponded exactly with the two men who, the day before, had had a ride with the pastor.

"On another occasion," Brother Bill continues, "I, my wife, our son, and a friend of ours were by car on our way to visit my parents. This was about three o'clock in the morning. It was still dark and the visibility was bad. Suddenly a mule appeared on the road in front of our car. Instinctively, I avoided the mule by going to the right in front of it. The normal reaction is otherwise to go to the left toward the middle of the road, as one does not know what it looks like at the side of the road. My friend, who sat next to me in the front seat, said: 'I know why you turned to the right instead of to the left. There was actually not, as you saw and thought, only one mule, but three after each other across the road. If you had tried to avoid the first one by going to the left, we would have hit one of the two others.' We stopped the car and praised God for protecting and keeping us safe in an unaccountable way.

"When we some hours later came to my parents' house, we first met my brother. The first thing he said was, 'What happened to you just before three o'clock this morning? The Lord woke me up ten minutes to three, and I felt that I should pray for you. At three o'clock I got such a peace and fell asleep in a calm and restful way.'

"When we had been at home for a while," Brother Bill continues, "I called my sister and even before I had time to say hello, she said, 'What happened to you about three o'clock this morning?' The same thing had happened to her as to my brother. She had waked up ten minutes to three, prayed for us, and then had fallen asleep with the assurance that the Lord really would keep his protecting hand over us.

"A couple of hours later my father came home from work. He began very early in the mornings and had already left before we arrived. The first thing he said before I had time to say anything was, 'I saw you this morning when you were on your way here. The Lord woke me up ten minutes to three. I also saw three horses appear in front of you, and I prayed that the Lord might help you out of that situation. I saw how you turned to the right in front of the horses and only just avoided smashing into them.'

"The only thing I could say to my father was," Brother Bill says, "you evidently didn't see the long ears. They were not horses, they were mules!"

Brother Bill laughs in a catching way and stops talking,

but there are many persons who have questions. Later Bible studies will deal more about each gift, but the most anxious questioners have to have answers immediately to their most burning questions. The participants help each other to answer. Somteimes Brother Bill answers, sometimes someone else.

"Do we receive the Baptism in the Holy Spirit at the same time as we get saved; that is, do we get everything on one occasion or are these two separate experiences?" someone asks, and Brother Bill answers: "The Bible teaches the born again experience and the Baptism of the Holy Spirit as two separate experiences, even if they may happen very close to each other in time. In the charismatic movement we often see this. Let me use an example which maybe makes the difference clear: The Spirit is as the tea in a teabag—when we get saved, we get the Spirit of God, which after that dwells in us as the tea in the teabag. When God's rivers of living water through the Baptism of the Holy Spirit flow through us, it happens as when you pour water on a teabag. The content comes out, gives off its color, and gives a flavor to those around. People can see it in our lives, in our actions, that we are baptized in the Holy Spirit! We get so much so we cannot keep it to ourselves any longer. The fruits of the Spirit grow ripe and are used! The Baptism in the Holy Spirit is the key to further blessings. Our souls have been opened to God's infinite blessings. And furthermore, the Baptism in the Holy Spirit is only the beginning! All gifts are for you besides the gifts of speaking the language of the angels."

"Is it possible to be baptized in the Holy Spirit without speaking in tongues?"

"Everyone who receives the Baptism in the Holy Spirit can speak in tongues, but for one reason or another, everybody does not use this gift. There has been and there is some confusion concerning this, but as far as I can see, it is Scriptural that everyone who receives the Baptism in the Holy Spirit also can speak in tongues if she or he wants to. The Lord does not force the speaking in tongues on us, but all the time we have our free will to use the gift or refrain from using it. The main point is, as Paul on several occasions points out, that speaking in tongues is used in wisdom."

"How many Spiritual gifts can *one* person have?"

"Nobody 'has,' 'owns,' a Spiritual gift, but if we are baptized in the Holy Spirit, God in his grace can use us for all the gifts. The gifts of the Spirit are not our own; we are only channels for them. We get what we believe. If we believe in being used for only one gift, we are used in only one, etc."

"Why do some people receive the Baptism in the Holy Spirit at the same time they ask for it while it seems to be so difficult for others to receive the baptism despite the fact that they have searched for it for a long time? Is not the promise meant for everybody? Are there exceptions?"

"The reasons why there are people who have searched for a long time without being able to receive are specifically two:

"Firstly, they have a preconceived opinion about how the Baptism in the Holy Spirit takes place, and they are searching for the vocal sign instead of the Baptism in the Holy Spirit itself; that is, they are searching for the speaking in tongues instead of the power to fulfill the work which the Spirit leads us to do. A Baptism in the Holy Spirit can never be forced upon somebody. It is a natural part and a continuation of the deep, inner joy of the conversion, yet independent of the feelings of the moment. It is something we can experience in the middle of the day—nothing occult or unnatural. The speaking in tongues is accordingly not the Baptism in the Holy Spirit, but an external manifestation, a vocal expression, for it.

Exactly as we in faith accept the salvation, we must in faith accept the Baptism in the Holy Spirit. When people seek the Baptism in the Holy Spirit, they believe that they have not gotten what they asked for because they did not speak in tongues at once. And therefore, they ask for it again and again, instead of thanking God in faith for what they have received. God's power is released through this act of faith. There are many examples of people who have asked for the Baptism in the Holy Spirit and in faith hold on to what they have received. Sometime later they have also used the gift of speaking in tongues!

"The second point, which is intimately connected with the first one, is that they expect God to do that part which God expects us to do. The Baptism in the Holy Spirit consists of two parts: God's part, when He fills us with His Holy Spirit and gives us the gifts; and our part, when we accept to be an instrument for the gifts of the Spirit and in faith speak out the language which God has given unto us. About the disciples on the first day of Pentecost we can read: 'And they were all filled with the Holy Ghost, and began to speak with other tongues, as the Spirit gave them utterance (Acts 2:4).' 'They were all filled'—God's part. 'And began to speak with other tongues'—the disciples' part. The Holy Spirit gave utterance, but they themselves opened their mouths and began to speak the language they had received.

"A common reason for people to doubt the speaking in tongues and keep it back is that they the first time only spoke some words. They are tempted to believe that it is not right, when the 'language of angels' does not rush forth. Many people have been in a similar situation, but have used the words they received, and gradually they get more and more.

"Some keep the speaking in tongues back because there are people who say that what they speak in tongues is something they studied before or something mystical, sub-conscious, or 'from the devil.' But we can be convinced that if we pray to God to give us the Holy Spirit, it is God through Jesus Christ who gives us what we ask about. 'If ye then, being evil, know how to give good gifts unto your children: how much more shall your heavenly Father give the Holy Spirit to them that ask him? (Luke 11:13).'"

With the prayer to become channels for the Holy Spirit and thereby to be real, living, warm persons by grace the participants of the Bible study group leave for their every-day chores. They go to the children's always inquisitive, changing world, to the husbands' and men's world full of ambition and stress, disappointment and success, to the wives' and women's calling as housewives or workers in a profession, to the happiness of the middle-aged years and later-on years, often threatened by reactive depressions—out to the "everyday" where all need love and loving. The everyday of life is not a "dance of roses." But all are con-vinced that this hour before God has given them visions to do everything better and better. They love life in a much more meaningful way.

CHAPTER 8

A Usual Weekday Evening
or an Unusual

A *usual* weekday evening: almost packed in the Chapel despite bad weather and rain. The feeling of a cold, humid evening in the autumn disappears inside the door of the Chapel when one sees the people. The singing in unison advances strongly and mightily up against the high ceiling in the old house in the park. The old open fire-places masoned by blocks of marble suck in the sound which also reaches through the ceiling and the wooden stairs into the upstairs halls. One can imagine the old paperhangings fluttering and the lamp globes and chandeliers swinging. As usual the singing is led in an inspiring way by one of the talented songleaders.

"We certainly like to sing here," the songleader says, "so let us sing 'His banner over us in love.' And let's do it with accompanying arm movements." They sing and form their arms and hands into symbols for the words in the song. This whole scene reminds one of a better world. It is filled with spontaneous happenings. One laughs with all his heart due to sheer happiness.

Very often it happens that people lift their hands while singing. This is nothing strange; it just happens. It must be a sign of engagement!

SOMEONE HAS A TESTIMONY

"Does someone have anything to tell?" the songleader asks.

A young man comes forward who is home from Bible school for a few days. With his entire face filled with smiles and dimples, he stands in front of one of the microphones and just looks happy for quite a while before he says, "Thank you all for all your prayers! Thank you for all love! Thank you for helping me find myself again and grow through the salvation in Jesus Christ. So many new faces I see here today! Many of you, I am sure, do not know me, but I am convinced you can join when I say 'God is good!' Thank you for all prayers!"

The songleader lays his one arm around the boy's shoulders, looks his straight in the eyes, and says, "I remember . . . I remember exactly what you are talking about. You said 'Yes' to the Lord when you were totally wrecked after having been on drugs for many years. As an influential gangleader you had, so they said, 'lighted up' your entire school. So many did you lead into using drugs that you were feared by teachers and parents—even by the school board. No one of them could recognize you if they saw you now. The transformation is unbelievable!"

What was not said publicly was that this boy had been so deeply disturbed and poisoned by drugs that it was medically considered necessary to keep him in a hospital for an unforeseeable length of time. He was living dead. He did not respond. Nobody gave him any hope. He had to be tended as if he were a helpless baby.

Only his mother and a few others believed that there still remained some hope. Their faith was like a strong warm wind of love. In that faith the mother brought her boy home, laid her hands on him according to the Scriptures, and prayed for him, proclaiming him healed in the name of the Lord. Nobody knows what happened then, but something happened—a miracle which became more obvious day by day. All consider his healing and rehabilitation to be a miracle. Now he is a student at the Bible school studying to become a minister.

A tall, nice-looking young lady comes forward. She usually does not talk about herself, not even privately. But now in an excuse-me manner she does just that. She tells quietly without gestures about God's guidance in her life. She tells how the Lord guided and kept and helped her up to date and how she really trusts in Him to lead her also in the future. Today she just wants to share her faith in God with all the people gathered in the Chapel this evening: "God is near in the daily life. God is here in the fellowship of prayer."

Her testimony is received by the people with joy and praises. The physician from the medical society whispers to us: "This girl is a colleague of mine. She is an intern at the university hospital."

When the doctor praising the Lord has finished her testimony, a man with a little wooden cross hanging around his neck now wants to say something. He asks for prayers for a relative who is having an especially difficult time, exactly like he himself had to go through just before he found the peace of God. All join hands and pray together to God for his intervention. One prays for everyone who has difficulties; one prays that they might find God's answers to their problems; and one prays especially for this man's relative.

Jesus says:

Again I say unto you, That if two of you shall agree on earth as touching any thing that they shall ask, it shall be done for them of my Father which is in heaven (MATTHEW 18:19).

SINGING LIKE PLAYING OF
TRUMPETS IN JERICHO

Many arise when they start to sing in unison, "Victory in Jesus." This song has become somewhat of a signature melody at the prayer meetings in the Chapel. It is as if the mortar-made decorations were shaking—these decorations which were made by skillful masons many years ago, and serve instead of wallpaper boards between the ceilings and the walls. But if Jericho's walls could fall from trumpet sounds, it is not remarkable if some mortar dust falls from the walls of the Chapel due to the intense and moving singing. In the engagement people start clapping hands to the singing. Others step out in the aisles and are coming forward singing. More and more people do so. Finally there are about twenty, mainly young people, who have come forward in the Chapel singing and now are walking in one line as in a victory march.

THE WINDS OF LOVE MAKE DRUG ADDICTS
FREE LIKE BIRDS

Similar expressions of participation in the service have been usual throughout the history of the church. For centuries, for example, on Palm Sunday worshippers have walked up to the altar in their churches singing, with branches of palm leaves in their hands. The offerings on mission days often have been given at the altar, preceded by a march by the congregation up to the altar, etc. The spontaneous expression of Christian worship which the young people today manifested in the Chapel is called a Jericho march.

First in the march we see a young man whom we know very well. He has told us his life's story, and he wants to share this story with everybody in the hope that it might be of help for at least a few.

Already as a 13-year-old boy he had started to spend

80

most of his time out on the streets. Together with other boys of his age and older he started to steal cars and commit burglaries. They were stealing everything they happened to run into. Like many of his friends, he was arrested several times. In spite of this, he continued as before. This gang became more and more involved and feared. Only whites were allowed to be members in his group. Four of his best teen-age years disappeared in constant and often bloody fights with black youngsters. He hated blacks in general and especially members of some black gangs, with which his group had these constant fights.

He became increasingly entangled. To "escape everything" he joined the army when he was seventeen. Two years later he went to Vietnam, and after a dreadful year there he came back to the United States filled with unpleasant memories. Again he began to join gangs which were involved in all sorts of criminality. His entire mind was filled with hatred and bitterness. Already in his early teens he had started on drugs, including alcohol, and at the age of twenty he was deeply disturbed by all these poisons. His LSD trips had been especially wrecking with difficult hallucinations for all senses. This broke him entirely, and he was referred to a mental institution. Before he was admitted he prayed to God, just by himself. He prayed about salvation through Jesus Christ. When he came to the examination for admission to the hospital, the doctors felt that the information given in the referral letter did not comply with their findings. He was already much better.

His recovery was speedy, thus it was not necessary to keep him in the hospital except for a short period of observation. When he was discharged from the hospital, he decided to start a new life in another part of the country. And this was really what happened. "By chance" he met some of the "Jesus people", he was "baptized in the Holy Spirit," "grew tremendously in the Lord" and developed into a veritable "elder in the Kingdom of God." At the Chapel he became one of the brethren serving at the communion table. There he walks now as an authentic mark of thanks to the Lord for His power to change lives. This boy had been set free from the weird poison of narcotics and from hatred and bitterness. All of these evils had been replaced by the love of God. He now seeks everything with new eyes and a new mind.

BEAUTIFUL GIRL IN AFRO-HAIR

While walking he turns around and smiles with his whole face toward a girl who walks behind him—a girl from another ethnic group, a girl in typical Afro-hair, with dark brown eyes filled with laughter, brown-black skin, and a mouthful of shining white teeth. This boy who earlier had always hated blacks now has a black "sister"! There is neither Jew nor Greek, black nor white—all are one in Jesus Christ.

The girl is a student at one of the colleges in the city. Not long ago she was a member of a militant organization, intensely hated the whites, and always carried a gun. Marijuana and confusion were part of her daily life. Young, angry, and used! Tough and impudent when she was among peers, she was crying when she was alone. She knew that what she was doing was wrong—entirely wrong. Hatred gave birth to hatred, and violence gave birth to suffering. But she was not able to free herself from this. In her despair she said, "God, if you exist, please help me." God existed!! In the same moment she prayed, she was filled with a feeling of happiness—a feeling which she distinctly registered. Sometime later she also experienced the Baptism of the Holy Spirit. She was alone in her room when it happened. As one of the hostesses at her college during a registration day of students, she had come to her room quite exhausted to rest a little while before an official welcoming party for the newcomers. She lay down on her bed and prayed to God to give her strength for the evening. She had never been to a service where people spoke about Baptism in the Holy Spirit. In fact she knew very little about it. But lying down on the bed as she prayed she started very naturally to speak in tongues!! At the same time she was filled with a pronounced feeling of peace, strength, and love. When this came into her heart, it was as if everything else in her were rinsed out. The fruits of the Holy Spirit since that day color this girl's life. She went back to school after she had met the Lord for salvation. Her studies became more and more successful. She has become one of the most popular students of her college, holds elected offices, and is employed on the campus. A black student holding elected offices in the student body of a college with mainly white students! This is an achievement which would have been difficult only a few years ago.

"The remarkable thing is," she says, "that God lately has sent so many new real people—black and white—my way. I love them all!" One who earlier "saw red" when she saw "white" now sees God's messengers in all.

WARM WINDS AT THE CAMPFIRE

Smiling and singing a young nice couple walks side by side in the Jericho march. They were both baptized in the Holy Spirit about a year ago during a tour to a camp for young Baptists in southern U.S.A. The young wife told us, "In the evenings we used to sit around a campfire and pray. One evening two girls left the rest of us to be by themselves for prayers. When they came back after a while, we saw that something had happened to them. They looked so tremendously happy, hugged us all, and showed us so much love! Most of the people on this camping tour knew about the Baptism in the Holy Spirit. My husband and myself, however, did not know about it, so we were wondering what was going on. All I knew was that I was not really right with God and that I was not happy at all. One of the girls at the camp obviously noted this, because one evening she came up to me, put one arm around my shoulder, and asked what it was that made me look unhappy. I started to cry. She called for the camp minister and we talked, and then he prayed with me for forgiveness of my sins. Then suddenly, without having prayed for it, I started to speak in tongues, and a wonderful happiness filled me.

"My husband, who at the time was still at the university a good way towards his graduation to become a teacher, was very much insulted. This was too much for his intellectualism. But twenty-four hours later he also was baptized in the Holy Spirit!

"The charismatic experience to us meant the beginning of new dimensions of Christian life. We have after this, for instance, been able to love everybody. A girl at my job, a secretary like me, whom I hated intensely, is now one of my best friends. The most remarkable part of my testimony is that when I was delivered from hate, my asthma, which I had suffered from for many years, disappeared!"

Just after this beautiful couple walks a young man in a tailor-made suit. It is uplifting to see how his eyes shine with happiness and with thankfulness for having been freed from the epidemic disease which tied him down so long—homosexuality. The miracle of salvation gave a new song to his heart, and new virility to his body. Salvation in Jesus Christ gave him power to flee—no, fly—back to reality!

THE SWEDISH BABY BROTHER

Marching also is a Swedish student. After studies in Upsala he had come to visit his elder brother who at that time was a student at one of the colleges in this city.

About six months earlier the elder brother had experienced a dramatic change when he had met the Lord and had been baptized in the Holy Spirit at a youth lunch which was part of a Christian conference. We have told his story in Chapter 2. The younger brother was very impressed by his brother's stability and living Christian testimony. In the plans for the summer the boys included Explo 72 in Dallas. Explo 72 was a training course in evangelization. About 100,000 mainly young Christians had preregistered, and still more came. What a crowd of Christian young people! The younger brother, to start with, felt as if he were outside of it all. He decided to go back to Sweden as soon as possible.

"I am going to hold out this week, then I'll go home," he thought. But something great happened to him! After three days at Explo 72 he had met so many real living people that he was fully convinced that the Christian faith would be the answer also for him, and he invited Jesus into his life.

He felt a peace and happiness which he had never felt before. This was the highlight of his life. As a continuation of the miracle which had already happened to him, he started to speak in tongues when he was thanking God for salvation on the following day. This did not scare him, for it came totally naturally. "It just came and filled my mouth," he says.

Similar religious experiences are testified to by many who participated in Explo 72, the purpose of which had been to train young people for evangelism. With the Holy Spirit they were given divine power to become witnesses for Christ!

HIGH SCHOOL KID RUNS AWAY BUT
COMES HOME AGAIN

Behind the young Swede we see an American boy who now is a senior in high school. He is one year older than most of his classmates because last year in school he messed it all up. He felt that he had to quit. He also wanted to leave his home, despite the fact that everything was all right there—no discussions, no trouble. But his friends, who lived on the same street, had started to smoke marijuana. The environment became contaminated. They started to speak bad things about each other's parents, to magnify small incidences in the past, and to blame everything but themselves for their problems, including unsuccessful tests in school. The pressure from his friends was intense, and he did not want to be a chicken. They had started to smoke marijuana now and then, but soon did it every day. It became difficult to find money for the larger and larger quantities which they, as a group, needed. They had to drive far away to buy what they wanted; and because of this they "crossed state lines" with drugs, which they sold to whomever paid the most. They began to not come home all weekend, and then not at all. And so they became "drop-outs" from school and "runaways."

Several months disappeared in one long marijuana intoxication, until one day they were arrested as drug pushers. At the police station the boy remembered what his father had repeatedly said a long time ago: "Whatever happens to you and wherever you are, if you are in a situation in which you are stuck, call me." In spite of the humiliation the boy called his father from the police station. With the next flight his father was on his way to the other corner of the United States to help his son, and if possible, to take him home.

The boy came home. He felt the warm winds of love at home and among Christian people. He realized where the real thing was to be found. In silence he prayed to

God to forgive him all his sins. In this silence he was saved and started to speak the language of the angels. He went back to school and became a straight-A student, which did not surprise him at all! "So clear in my head as I became in the moment I received the Holy Spirit can only be explained as a healing, a healing of my mind and character—a miracle," he says. "I had not been able to think one logical thought for a long time! But 'lightning' from heaven cleared up my brain, and then I started to function again." No wonder he is happy. Tears of joy fill his eyes. His thankfulness to the Lord is obvious. He is grateful to the Lord for his new freedom, freedom from chemically caused short circuits in his brain!!

ALSO THE GOOD BOYS GET STRENGTH THROUGH THE WARM WINDS OF LOVE

Just behind "the son who was lost, but now is found," walks a 17-year-old boy who always looks especially happy. He is a senior in high school, too. He comes regularly to the Chapel but also to his own church—a large Baptist church. He has grown up in a Christian family and has had an almost entirely problem-free childhood, unlike many other boys and girls now coming to the Chapel. As a natural product of spiritual growth, the gifts of the Spirit were seen in him. Through his frankness he has been a great blessing in his school. If his schoolmates spoke up about their beliefs, he did so about his. He spoke to everybody—students and teachers, the principal included. He got the principal's approval to start a prayer group at the school. In this prayer group regular revival meetings were held, and many of his schoolmates were saved and filled with the Spirit.

ENGAGED

Marching also are a boy and a girl who are going to be married soon right here in the Chapel. About a year ago when they found God, they also found each other in a new way. They discovered new dimensions in each other —dimensions which made stronger their affection and tenderness toward each other. They found that they both were praying for "God's guidance" in their lives as never before. They both became a great blessing to people in their capacities as artists in renowned gospel groups. What a year of new blessings! What a beautiful way of preparing for a marriage! They were on the road to many places, gave many concerts, and above all led many, many to the Lord. A beautiful couple in a charming victory march!!

CHARISMATIC CATHOLIC

A quiet Catholic college graduate also enjoys the march. His major subject is sociology. Two years ago he met some Jesus people, was saved, and one week later he was baptized in the Holy Spirit. He has always had an "intellectual disposition" and he can scarcely be called "emotional."

"But it does not matter," he says. "The Baptism in the Holy Spirit does not depend upon how much or how little emotional you are." He radiates peace and love. The source of this peace and love is obvious: God through the charismatic renewal. This young Catholic man is richly used by God to speak prophetic words of blessing and edification for the entire congregation!

This whole scene is indescribably beautiful and real. We took many photos of it in our memories. It is a striking contrast to marches of other origins. There are no posters, no slogans filled with hatred, no fights, only love, peace, open hands, and pure hearts, each with a song of praises to the living God—a song written in joyous faces.

The marchers return to their seats, and Brother Richard comes to one of the microphones to give a personal testimony. He says that his opinion about healing changed after his charismatic experience. "Earlier I believed that God could heal, but that He only did it through physicians. Now I know that God can heal also when doctors have given up. I believe that God can heal anybody—today. I have seen so many healings recently, also in my own family, that I cannot doubt it anymore."

PILOT WITH NEW WINGS

The place is filled with faith. Somebody starts to sing "Only believe, only believe, all things are possible, only believe." Some proceed forward spontaneously for special prayers. A couple of men almost immediately stand up and also come forward to help pray with these. One of the men is the young man who a few minutes ago had been first in the Jericho march. Another is the physician from the medical society. He believes in prayers in both big and small things and willingly prays like a brother together with his sisters and brothers in the Lord. We know him already from prayer meetings at the Chapel. We also know how careful he always is to point out to people: "See your physician. Have a medical checkup." The reason to follow such words of wisdom he feels is self-explanatory!

Among the men who come forward to help in counseling and prayers is a man who himself has experienced a divine healing. He is a slightly crook-backed man in his 40's with a long black beard and long, dark hair. He is one of the personalities in the Chapel.

As a young man he had joined the Air Force. While serving abroad he was struck by inflammation of the muscles around the spine, and after much pain and many and long hospitalizations, he ended up in a veterans' hospital in the southern United States. In spite of intensive treatments his condition got worse, and he became a bedridden invalid. Parallel to the muscle inflammation which

89

bent his back, an inflammation of the left hipjoint increased to such a degree that he could not walk. In the meantime, he lost his wife and daughter through divorce. When we met this man, he had not seen his child in more than ten years. But he could walk!! And he was an important father-figure for many of the young folks in the Chapel—a spiritual pillar in God's house.

The miracle in his life happened about three years ago. He was at that time entirely bedridden. An operation of his hip was suggested. In this situation he rededicated his life to the Lord and experienced forgiveness and peace. His religious renewal changed his attitudes. He became happy and outgoing and felt convinced that God was able also to make him healthy in his body. That is why he one day stood up in faith and started to walk. At first it was a little bit shaky, but by and by he walked better and better. Soon he was discharged from the hospital, and after a while he was able to start working. He was extremely excited about this and thankful to the Lord, praising Him with all his heart. In the midst of this praise the Lord filled him with the Spirit, and he started to speak in tongues. He now helps the sick in prayers as they are coming forward.

An elderly, well-dressed, elegant woman is among those who come first for prayers. The following day she has an appointment in a physician's office. She has some difficulties in one leg, and she wants her sisters and brothers at the Chapel to pray with her. Before offering prayers, Brother Bill tells about a healing which took place recently. A housewife in her early thirties a few weeks earlier had come for special prayers. She had difficulties of different types. Her marriage was on the verge of falling apart. She wanted to leave her husband because he had been baptized in the Holy Spirit, and had become acutely depressed and unhappy. Another problem was that her endocrine system was not in balance. During five years she had not had her period. Furthermore, she had just discovered that she had "lumps" in both breasts. In the midst of all this, she had broken a toe and had difficulty walking.

In this condition one evening she came to the Chapel. She was totally taken by the love and understanding she met. Everybody prayed for her, above all that she should be filled with peace in her heart and that her marriage should be healed. When all prayed she felt that she was able to leave everything in God's hands. She regained physical balance. The pain in her toe disappeared at the same time. All this gave her faith for God's healing powers also for the lumps in her breasts and for her failing periods. She prayed, and a miracle took place. The lumps in her breasts disappeared! Furthermore, a week later she started her first period in five years!! This miracle points to a deep relationship between religious experiences and the hormonal system and glands. There are many testimonies of similar nature.

Now the lady with the sore leg bows her head for prayers. "I want us all to take part in these prayers and as many as possible in the laying on of hands," Brother Bill says. "If we do it that way no one will say that Brother Bill or somebody else here has the power of healing. God is the one who heals. I do not have a special gift to pray with the sick. I only stand here like you, praising God for what is happening. We are all invited to be channels for all of God's gifts." Many lay hands on the lady's shoulders, and the others join hands as they pray—no long prayers, only a few words to the point, and in assurance that nothing is impossible for God.

A great many people have been prayed with, when a young man comes forward. He says, "Please pray for me that I might receive the Baptism in the Holy Spirit." In

91

this service the Baptism in the Holy Spirit had not been mentioned. But that does not mean that such a need cannot develop anyway!!

The people around him lay their hands on the boy's shoulders and start praying. Not even a minute later the boy gloriously testifies to the charismatic experience! And to the word from the Bible: "And all things, whatsoever ye shall ask in prayer, believing, ye shall receive" (Matthew 21:22).

There has been no altar call in the traditional sense in this service—no begging or forcing. Spontaneously people have come forward. In the middle of the ongoing meeting people have found salvation and received the Baptism in the Holy Spirit.

Now they join hands in thanksgiving to the Lord for this day. They sing, "Give the Glory to Jesus," and as they sing they start hugging and greeting each other. It is like a big family, although each returns to a different address.

It is raining hard outside, but that is like a small drip compared with the heavenly showers now falling all over the world—showers which have been falling on people in prayers this *unusual* weekday evening.

CHAPTER 9

We All Need Help Sometimes

AN UNHAPPY STORY

A group of businessmen who meet in a Bible study and prayer group once a week wanted to do something special for the many outcast young people who, cheated of their ambitions and cracked inside, live in the undervegetation of the drug culture. Like cars smashed to wrecks in drag-racing and motor cross-competitions, these young people are thrown out as junk by the drug millionaires—these, the actual gangsters of our modern-day society. The victims offer such undesirable public relations for what is peddled that they have to be passed out of sight, these gangsters think. But this is not what our dedicated Christian men thought that a merciful God would allow. They found a house where some of these people could stay for a while. This place really became a place of God. Many were saved there.

The following is one of many examples of how the atmosphere of love which came to dominate this place influenced a young man:

"I grew up in a good home," he tells us. "No problems at home during the years when I grew up. I had lots of friends all around. But I felt lonely anyway. I did not have any close friends. This, however, I would be able to compensate for one day! I had already made up my plans for the future: When I had graduated from school, I was going to be a singing star and make lots of money and many friends. I had always been weak for money. As early as at the age of six I worked summertime to make money. Later on I worked on tobacco plantations in spite of being allergic to the tobacco leaves. But I worked through all hurdles, if only I made some money.

"I reached my goal and became a singer. Like so many others, I started to smoke marijuana without really intelligently thinking about what I was going into. It was given to me free. If I had had to pay, my covetousness would have kept me from starting," the boy says with a certain degree of self-irony. "But quite soon I was tired of the type of life that I lived. The same things every day—marijuana, music, sex.

"One Wednesday evening a friend of mine told me about Jesus and that Jesus loved me. I almost did not know who Jesus was, and I did not know that he loved me. The following evening I happened to be free, and of all things, I went to a prayer meeting! This was held in an old house. The house had been converted to a place for boys and girls who earlier had been on drugs. There were many different people there, also a boy whom I knew, a former member of a feared motorcycle gang. It was a silent, peaceful atmosphere in that house. Entirely unemotionally the same evening I invited Jesus into my life. He accepted my invitation! The feeling of joy which in that moment filled me made me cry. I cried as probably never before in my life. When crying and praying, I was filled with the Holy Spirit, and I started to speak in tongues. Nobody had mentioned anything to me about this before; I did not know a thing about the Holy Spirit and speaking in tongues. It just came to me."

It is just about two years ago since this happened. All of the unselfish love the young man has met since that day among his new brothers and sisters of all ages, Christian brothers and sisters, has been wonderful. "Earlier my love always was tied to conditions—I love you *if* you do that or that for me, or *if* I get that or that. Now everything is without conditions. I try to give others what I have received myself." He cannot talk enough about what a great influence Christian people who cared and do care for him in reality have had and now have on him.

This boy has been a great blessing for many! Together with three other young people, he has traveled a great deal and visited many schools with programs of testimonies and singing. He saw many of his schoolmates being saved and filled with the Spirit. Later he was accepted at a Bible college as a student in order to reach a deeper knowledge of God's word "so that I can give of this when I testify."

"When I think back on the time I lived in the house which my brethren, the businessmen, sponsored, it is with a deep feeling of thankfulness," he says. "We really learned what humbleness and love between people is. Now I know what it is to be each other's servants."

GIRL WITH NO NAME—A RUNAWAY

The willingness to help others sometimes takes dramatic and unexpected expressions. Brother Bill one day received a telephone call from two despairing parents. They had learned that their daughter, who had been a runaway from home since a long time ago, had been seen in the same city as Brother Bill lives. This is a metropolitan area of half a million people. They did not know where the girl stayed but assumed that she lived in the drug subculture someplace. Brother Bill prayed to God to lead him as he went out to try to find the girl, for this was certainly not an easy project. Soon he learned that the girl was using a false name—a usual manner in this drug world so full of lies. Besides, this name changing seems to indicate a constant desire to be able to escape from it all as anonymously as possible. The only identification Brother Bill had of the girl was her parents' description of her. He had never met her.

In an astonishing way he came in contact with persons who were able to help him, each one a little bit, in his difficult task as a detective. Surprisingly soon he found the girl. Brother Bill knew what he was going to say to the girl when he found her. He had known it all the time. It was what the girl's parents had said to Brother Bill over the telephone: "We love her soooo!" These words were just the words Brother Bill said when he soon found her: "Your parents love you soooo!!" These words opened the girl up. She left everything and returned home, where everything went well both immediately and afterwards. Everything was transformed through this testimony of forgiveness and love.

With so many runaways and lost kids and so many everywhere without a home, Christian friends have had their eyes opened to the great importance of inviting and receiving into their homes people who have invited Jesus into their lives. Such invitations have especially been offered young people who are recuperating from the poisoning of narcotics and who have left home, school, or work. Now they get a new home and, thereby, the support they need at least during the first months of rehabilitation. After having left old friends, they are able to grow in the faith in this new environment. It is a usual phenomenon. But charismatics feel as if they have responsibilities like parents to all of God's children and the young people who, by God's guidance, are coming their way.

It is exciting to see how much these new models mean in influencing an altered behavioral pattern and to see how the young are changed in what they do and how they do it, and in what they say and how they say it, through these fine Christian fathers and mothers of different ages.

THE ACTRESS

After a year in college a girl had dropped out to go to Hollywood to try to become an actress. This had always been her dream. She was good looking and had great ambitions, but in Hollywood there were many other girls with the same good looks and ambitions. Through lectures in acting, talent hunts, and parties, she started to get "contacts." However, she did not make any money and was quite poor. To make money to support herself she applied to become a commercial airline hostess and was accepted. At the same time she worked hard to get a chance as an actress, but her efforts to be discovered led her on the wrong track and to people who took advantage of her. She became increasingly disgusted with all the parties to which she had been falsely lured in her attempts to be discovered. She had not been strong enough to say "No, thank you" to champagne and other drinks, and she had soon become dependent upon drugs and alcohol. When she noticed this, she really sensed how false all this was. She was on the verge of suicide.

She now thanks the Lord because just at that time she learned about a successful Christian actor and singer who always had an open house! A place where God lived! The girl went to the actor's and his wife's home. There she met people who really cared about her as a human being. She got a new home but she also came "back home to the Lord." Of course, it took some time to untangle all the nets in which she was caught—her old "friends" hunted her—but she was free forever through God's love and Spirit. The Spirit was such a reality for her that she could not get over it: this praising of the Lord in new languages. It was so simple but had such deep meaning.

By and by she also got many new friends who helped her without thinking about earthly rewards. The girl herself has been able, through work in a Christian bookstore, to pay back to others something of what the Christian people in Hollywood did for her when she needed help. And now she says, "We all need help sometimes." Help and love: love like water from the mountains for the one who is thirsty, love like bread for the one who is hungry.

THE CAR MECHANIC

"God has given us lots of different talents in lots of different areas," a quiet car mechanic about forty years old said as usual with both feet on the ground. "I, for instance, have got the gift to be practical. It is fun to work with engines, and I think it is especially gratifying to repair cars.

"I understand cars, hear if the engine runs right or wrong and know what has to be done. This I have told friends and neighbors and people in different prayer groups. Thereby I have been able to help many to save both time and money. It is expensive to have a car repaired, and there are people who cannot afford it—especially for single ladies, widows, and divorcees with children, a steep car repair bill can be difficult to meet. God has given me great blessings for this."

For whosoever shall give you a cup of water to drink in my name, because ye belong to Christ, verily I say unto you, he shall not lose his reward (MARK 9:41).

We all need help sometimes even if we are not hungry and thirsty. Just the solicitude is worth more than one can measure.

SCANDINAVIAN MISSIONARY

An old Scandinavian missionary is traveling through on

98

her way to her mission field. She has prayed to God to guide her to meet the right persons at the right time during her travels and her stopovers at different places. And she has above all prayed that the Lord might open doors for her to find some suitable gifts for her friends in the mission field. She gives her testimony in a prayer meeting and also in the Chapel and tells about the many very poor members in the big church at the mission field. Then somebody gets the idea of bringing some used, but good, dresses and suits for the missionary to take with her to her friends. She cannot stay but one and a half weeks in the city. During that time everybody seems to bring old clothing for the missionary—clean, fine, and if necessary, mended clothing. On the day of her departure about four hundred pounds of clothing in well-packed boxes were delivered to the bus station. Besides the boxes, there was also money to cover the freight!

A NEW FAMILY WITH MANY MEMBERS

She is a young divorced girl with a little daughter. Her former husband seldom sends money for their child. She is ambitious and works as much as she possibly can besides her college studies. While the young mother works or studies, many of her Christian friends take turns babysitting. The care also includes food and clothing. One day a good supply of groceries and clothing arrived—gifts from heaven, the young mother felt! This gift from persons who had said "Yes" to the commandment about love between all is a testimony about the Gospel in action!

A lady in a prayer group had said that she did not like Jews. She never had and would probably never have done so if she had not met a Jewish couple at a prayer meeting. She did not meet these people just socially. She met them in the fellowship of mutual prayers and devotion and happiness in God. The lady could not but love them—love them to a degree that she was even able to help in a special need. All her prejudices toward Jews disappeared. Fellowship in prayers and giving of herself solved for her this very difficult social problem.

It is usual that physicians, lawyers, and other professionals donate their services to persons in need. But to see men go so far in their help for the rehabilitation of so many—as these men we met in the prayer groups do—is fascinating. They do not hesitate to be on duty day and night, since they know that difficulties do not always come during ordinary office hours. For the clients to know this may be just that sign of extra care these people need to dare to seek help in circumstances of frustration and trouble.

There are many similar testimonies about genuine help. We have not tried to indicate that helping each other is not to be found in other groups of people. What we want to show is only that the fellowship is not limited only to the church service or the prayer meeting and that the help these people give each other is not only of a spiritual nature.

100

CHAPTER 10

"Ye Shall Be Witnesses"

But ye shall receive power, after that the Holy Ghost is come upon you: and ye shall be witnesses unto me both in Jerusalem, and in all Judaea, and in Samaria, and unto the uttermost part of the earth.   ACTS 1:8

In interview after interview the truth in this Bible verse has been confirmed. "When I was baptized in the Holy Spirit, I received power and the frankness to testify to others," is what many persons in the charismatic movement repeatedly told us. The charismatic movement has been: "a breaking of new land," "winning others for the Lord," "Christianity in action Sundays and weekdays."

THE RETREAT

A remarkable movement within the old denominations and a movement in which the charismatics have been of a tremendous blessing is the so-called laywitness mission. Laywitness missions started in the United States in the beginning of the 1960's, first within the Methodist church and later in the Episcopal and Presbyterian and other churches.

The laywitness mission has grown by and by and now plays an important role in the movement of spiritual renewal among its individual members, as well as for the entire membership of these denominations. Laywitness missions are usually held over a long weekend from Friday evening to Sunday afternoon. Missions are open to entire families or for women only or men only. Usually one or more special speaker is invited at these occasions to testify about his Christian experience. Quite a few of the professional men and also some of the women in the prayer groups and/or in the Chapel are often called as speakers or leaders at such meetings.

THE CONSTRUCTION WORKER—
A SPEAKER IN DEMAND

A construction worker in his upper thirties is one such speaker constantly in demand. He was saved in a laywitness mission, and after his charismatic experience about three years ago, he has participated as a speaker in about fifty such meetings. Just before his salvation he had joined a Methodist church "because of his family." He had continued, however, to do what he had done his entire grown-up life of about 20 years and like so many of his friends at work did—every weekend he intoxicated himself in drinking orgies. His alcoholic intake on weekends was copious.

When he had been a member of his church for three weeks, most of the men in the church were planning to go to a retreat in a motel out of town. They also invited him. He was not at all interested but, because it brought some prestige with it, he accepted the invitation. Secretly he thought that in some way he would be able to break his promise to go. The meeting started on a Friday evening; however, that evening he celebrated as usual. He came home intoxicated very late and thus could not go that evening. A couple of other men had been delayed too for different reasons. One of them had called and said that there would be a carload of men going out to the retreat

102

early Saturday morning, so they would come and pick him up at seven o'clock. His wife set the alarm clock to ring at 6:00 A.M.—a usual time for her husband to get up on weekday mornings, but not Saturday mornings when he often had a hangover.

Saturday morning came. The alarm clock rang, and our friend jumped up. Swearing that he was stupid to have promised to go, he still shaved, dressed, had breakfast, packed a suitcase, and was just ready to leave when the men from the church came at seven o'clock.

All the time on the way out he was protesting within himself. Having arrived at the motel, he immediately went up to his room, lay down on his bed, and slept for several hours—exactly what he had been doing most other Saturdays for twenty years! Late in the afternoon he woke up, dressed, and went down to "sit off" a couple of group sessions. Soon he felt that all this was fascinating. There he heard men testify about God's being with them in their jobs weekdays, how God helped them also with small things, and how new and meaningful life had become in this new dimension. Even their wives and children had improved, they felt. In reality all was as before. They lived in the same house. They had the same job. But in spite of this, everything was new. They fulfilled everything much better after having given their lives to God.

In the evening all participants met in one big seminar in a chapel close to the motel. During the day they had been divided into several smaller groups with ten to twelve persons in each group. "What a good meeting," he felt— "terrific speakers." Farmers, construction workers, taxi drivers, businessmen, people like himself were speaking.

After the evening service he and a couple of other men went for a walk. They spoke all the time about the Lord and they ended their walk in the chapel for prayers. The construction worker prayed in the chapel—really prayed

—for the first time he could remember. Sincerely he prayed: "God, if you think you have any use for a wretch like me, here I am. I give everything to you." In that moment he felt as if a current of electricity flowed from head to foot.

He says that he never since has taken alcohol and that he has "not been swearing but once." He did not particularly pray to be free from his drinking habit for he had not seen his drinking bouts as a problem—only "in passing" he also was set free from his alcoholic habit. His needs for stimulants were sufficiently met through the reality in Christ!

About two months later the construction worker and his wife were called to give their testimonies at a lay-mission conference. They had never before in their lives addressed an auditorium, but they did not feel nervous at all in this. They were asked to be the first two speakers at a breakfast meeting. They spoke about twenty minutes each, and their testimonies were instruments of great blessings to many present.

Afterwards the construction worker and his wife were standing together with a new friend and his wife at the altar in the chapel where these joint meetings were held. Everything seemed so beautiful to him, and he felt happy as never before in his entire life. While he was standing there looking at the altar, he felt that he saw a cross—a stirring, beautiful, empty cross. "Such bright colors," he thought, and pointed toward what he saw. But the others did not see the cross. Perhaps this was a reflection in the chapel window; perhaps it was a vision. For him anyway this experience became a special sign of God's grace toward him!

During the morning and at lunch he talked more with his new friend about God's grace. About two o'clock they had prayer together. His friend started to speak in tongues, and the construction worker, who never before had heard speaking in tongues, also started to do so at about the same time.

Ever since this experience our construction worker and his wife have been speakers at many laywitness meetings and weekend conferences within the Methodist church and other denominations. No one is afraid of them because they are baptized in the Holy Spirit. On the contrary! Many come to them for prayers. This layman and his wife have been praying with so many that they do not remember them all now. By the way, why count? God does that. The main thing is that we are his instruments. Once they prayed for a 30-year-old man to whom they had not even mentioned the phrase "Baptism in the Holy Spirit"; neither had the man ever heard speaking in tongues. They prayed for some other needs he had. In the middle of the prayer, this man started to pray in tongues. He did not know what this was until the construction worker afterwards explained it to him!

Persons who know the construction worker say that he not only has become a more effective member of his church, he has also become a better member of his professional team and his union—in all, a better citizen.

FREE FROM CURSING

A physician who is very active in laywitness missions told us the following: "When it comes to my experiences in the laywitness movement in my church and others, I first of all want to make it clear that any experience I may have had counts for nothing in life unless it points to Jesus. The only thing my experience is good for in relating the life of somebody else is to hold up a mirror in which my brother will see his need for Jesus.

"From the time I was seven years old, when a 'friend' taught me to use profanity, I was a real 'garbage mouth.'

The name of Jesus and his Father were frequently on my lips—but not in prayer! I had tried for years in vain to stop.

"One night as I sat in my library reading I took a Bible and read in Galatians, the 5th chapter, about the works of the flesh. In that moment I saw all of that which Paul describes as actually or potentially in myself—I saw none of the fruits of the Spirit. But through reading, I realized that Jesus loved me anyway. Seated in my favorite chair in the quietness of the library, I surrendered everything to Him. From that moment three and a half years ago, not only has no profanity, not even one, crossed my lips, a profanity has not even entered my mind. What my own efforts during many years and my prayers couldn't do, Jesus Christ accomplished in me in an instant as a free gift of His grace. It's impossible to understand, but it's real.

"I have often shared this experience in order to point to Jesus. I remember how a young pharmacist and his wife saw Jesus through this testimony when I was at a meeting for physicians, dentists, and pharmacists and their wives. Later that night the pharmacist and his wife were led to surrender their lives to Jesus, and now they are baptized in the Holy Spirit and very active in the laywitness mission.

"We were born again through Jesus Christ. In one moment this miracle of new birth takes place. As a physician I can't explain this. It is and it remains a divine miracle."

WRITINGS IN NEON LIGHTS

One of the many personalities in the Chapel, a lady who has meant a lot there, is an often-used speaker in lay-witness missions. She has told us about one such meeting: "I was very well prepared. In my preparation I had studied

106

quite a few appropriate books and equipped myself with quotations from these books—quotations which illustrated my thoughts. I wrote down points from my well-organized speech—at least I thought it was—with capitals on big cue cards. When I went up to the rostrum and looked at my cue cards, I could not see what I had written down. I was almost panicky. 'Help me, Lord,' I prayed within me. The answer came in a remarkable and surprising way! The Lord did not put the words in my mouth, but wrote them as if in neon lights in front of me. Short simple sentences with a very simple message about God's love. I felt the presence of the Lord so real that even today, a long time afterwards, I do not understand what happened.

"Many, many persons afterwards came to thank me and tell me what a blessing this had been to them. I told them just as it was, how I had prepared myself, and what had happened when I came up on the rostrum.

"The Lord wants to use us His way! He taught me to be more dependent on Him and His things . . . 'Which things also we speak, not in the words which man's wisdom teacheth, but which the Holy Ghost teacheth' (1 Corinthians 2:13a)."

DOOR-TO-DOOR WITNESSING

One day a group of young men decided to go more regularly to talk with people about the Lord, and not use only the opportunities coming up at random. They meet every Monday evening, have prayers, and then go out to witness. One of the most eager to come into that group, Brother Richard, tells us a little bit about the organization of this work and the results seen through it: "We usually go two by two when we do our home visits. At those visits we see persons with whom we earlier have had some contact, or whom we have been asked by a relative or some other person to visit. We also visit hospitals. People usually appreciate that we come, and it seems as if everyone is open for the Word these days.

"When I talk with people, I usually ask a couple of questions which I found in a book. Personally I find them very good. First we talk about general things. Then we ask if they will allow us to ask a couple of questions, and tell them that the questions will concern people's relationship to God. Up to now nobody has refused to let us ask our questions. The first is, 'Are you sure that you now are living in such a way that you are ready to meet God?' Whatever their answer is we proceed to the next question: 'If you stand in front of God and He asks you why He would consider you ready, what would be your answer?' On this last question we get lots of answers. For instance: 'I go to church.' 'I do as well as I can.' 'I try to follow the Ten Commandments.' When they have answered, we usually ask if they mind knowing what we would answer if we stood in front of God and were asked the same question. If they say go ahead, which everyone up to now has said, we give a short personal testimony about our experience of salvation through Jesus Christ, and we point out that only Jesus through His intervening suffering and blood makes us ready. Many then ask us questions and we get the opportunity to talk further. It is necessary to give people a chance to open themselves up. And it is important to take a real interest in them and try hard to understand—in love.

"When people see our concern for them, they open up their hearts, and we get a better chance to lead them to Jesus. Many have given their lives to Jesus this year through this work. I do not think I am exaggerating when I say that three out of four of the ones to whom we have testified have accepted Jesus as their Lord and Saviour.

"Some of us had just paid a visit to a man in a hospital in this city. When we walked out through the hall and stopped at the elevator, a black man was standing there. We gave him a tract. We turned around to wait for the elevator when the Lord said to one of us, 'You have the time to testify to this man also.' So we approached him. He had already started to read the tract. We asked him our questions and told him about salvation through Jesus Christ as a free gift. After five minutes' talk he said 'Yes' to the Lord. We were standing in the hallway holding hands, and there the man asked Jesus to come into his life.

"On another occasion we visited a married couple's house. They are both in their early forties. They had been to the Chapel a couple of times, but they were not Christians and did not have a church background. The husband was not at home when we came, but his wife was. We were standing on her doorstep; we had a nice conversation. She was very interested in knowing more about the Lord—so interested, it seemed to us as if she had just been waiting for anyone to come and show her how to be saved. There we stood and prayed as she accepted the Lord. A few months later the husband was hospitalized, and there alone in his hospital room he prayed to the Lord and gave his life to Him. I am convinced that his wife's decision for Christ led this man to the Lord. What a beautiful chain reaction a testimony can start!

"Another time we visited a lady and her teen-age daughter. They had been to the Chapel a couple of times. The mother was a Christian; the daughter was not. The girl sat down on the floor while we talked. It was moving to see how fascinated she was about what we related. She grabbed at every word. When I asked her if she wanted to be saved, she said 'Yes' immediately without hesitation. Just there, sitting on the floor, she accepted Jesus."

HITCHHIKERS

"When on the road in the car many opportunities are

given to talk to people about God by inviting hitchhikers for a ride. The reason why I give hitchhikers a ride is just because it gives me a chance to testify," Brother Richard says, "To get a good conversation going, already when I have stopped to pick them up, I usually say jokingly, 'Jump in if you are not afraid—I am a preacher?' This immediately gives them a notion of what they may expect. Not long ago I stopped to give a hitchhiker a ride—a young man. It was in the evening and we were on our way home from a hospital visit. The boy just wanted a ride for a couple of miles, so we did not have time to talk very much. When we arrived at the place where he had planned to leave, we stopped at the side of the road and continued our conversation for a little while, with the boy's permission and interest. Before the boy left the car he wanted us to pray together. He wanted to give his life to God. He wanted to be saved!"

These people testify to their fellowman because they know that the Gospel of Jesus Christ can "transform" a person totally and give them something to live by. The Gospel gave the answer to these witnesses, and every one of them believes that this Gospel is the answer also for others.

" . . . Ye shall be witnesses. . . ." (ACTS 1:8)

A YOUNG FRENCH GIRL

This is another example of how the great commandment to be witnesses works: A young French girl—a college student—had Christian friends who tried to share their glory in Jesus with her. She tells us the following: "I tried it my way. I had tried to find the truth and the purpose in life through studying psychology and philosophy and also through narcotics. For a little while I also investigated meditation and Eastern religions. I understood that nothing in all these had an answer for me. But I did not want to admit that Jesus was the answer. Oh, I had known all the time who He was—I knew it through the life of my grandmother who is a Christian and through other people from the prayer groups who actually, together with my grandmother, had prayed for me. But I refused to listen to Christians when they tried to testify to me. I got nervous when people talked about Jesus because I felt that there was a power in that name which I could not explain. Deep within me I knew that I could not run away from God all my life.

"One day I visited a Christian girl whom I knew well. We had tried 'pot' together before she was saved. This time she talked to me all morning. She talked about her new life and the real love she felt through Jesus Christ. It was this love I was looking for to its fullest degree. Later that afternoon I went back to her without knowing why. I was sort of led there. My friend then asked me if I wanted to pray and if I wanted to invite Christ into my heart. And I thought, 'I have tried everything else, so why not give Jesus a real chance!' I prayed an honest prayer. Jesus became Lord in my life! Three days later I was baptized in the Holy Spirit. What a happiness! God has by and by opened my eyes to see the truth about myself so that I always can be myself. He has healed me completely and has given me real and unselfish love to all people."

After running away from herself and from God, God found her through Jesus Christ, who took her in His arms. There she found herself as many others have done—many, many, whose testimonies we know. Some of these are related in this report.

Oh, yes: Ye shall be witnesses!

111

PART III

A Crude Analysis of Data

CHAPTER 11

Social and Other Characteristics of Charismatics Supported by Examples

The movements of spiritual awakening have a long and exciting history, often difficult to interpret. The "charismatic movement"—a revival in our days—forms the latest chapter in this history. The question is to determine if the Christian faith has ever been stronger among its confessors and if the Christians have ever before been more fervent in their beliefs and in so many corners of the world at one time as now.

Thousands of prayer groups have been born in many homes all over the world in only a few years, and new ones are born every day.

One of the places where charismatic people in the area in which we chose to take a closer look met was in a house which got the nickname, "The Chapel." We have earlier in this book told the story of the Chapel.

The activities in the Chapel started just two years ago, and for many of those who participated in the fellowship, the breaking of bread, and the prayers there, the experience of the fullness through the Holy Spirit coincides with this start. A great many of those who have come for worship to the Chapel since its inception report that they were baptized in the Holy Spirit between one and two years ago. Many give a later date but only a few say that they were baptized in the Holy Spirit more than three years ago.

This and other information in this chapter is based on interviews with people who have come to the prayer groups in different houses and/or to the meetings at the Chapel.

To maintain order in our interviews we constructed a questionnaire which we followed when we talked with people or which they themselves completed. We also interviewed many of those who completed the questionnaire on their own. The questions were about the significance of the charismatic experience for the interviewee and the social relationship in which they lived and worked.

PEOPLE STARTED TO PRAY ABOUT RICHER SPIRITUAL EXPERIENCES

Facts about true changes in other people's lives through the Baptism in the Holy Spirit are referred to in many of the testimonies in this study as to how people came to understand the blessings of the charismatic movement and started to pray for richer spiritual experiences for themselves, too. Some had been faithful churchgoers for many years but did not feel satisfied. They had been asking for something more in religion without actually knowing what this something was. They had started to pray by themselves, and there in their chambers the miracle of Pentecost happened to them. They had never been in a prayer meeting where someone had experienced the Baptism in the Holy Spirit—they had just seen these changes in other persons' lives—so they did not follow any given pattern when praying. They simply prayed without any preconceived pattern for it or without any previous indoctrination about how to be baptized in the Holy Spirit. And it happened! It changed their lives too!! Previous indoctrination in some cases that the experience by the apostles at the first day of Pentecost was just a one-time happening was not of any hindrance to these people's receiving of the Baptism in the Holy Spirit in 1973. Yet in the middle of their honest

116

prayers they experienced the Baptism in the Holy Spirit and praised God for it in other tongues!

A woman who is a member of an Episcopalian church told us the following: "I prayed by myself and received the Baptism in the Holy Spirit. I did not know what had happened, but I suddenly felt a strong inner joy, a euphoria, which I could not explain. A few weeks later I told an Episcopal priest about this. He explained to me that I had been baptized in the Holy Spirit. Some time later when I was alone in prayer at home, I began to speak in tongues, which I felt was a confirmation of what had happened."

Another lady—she is a member of a Presbyterian church—described her Baptism in the Holy Spirit as follows: "I had started to read the Bible a little more often than earlier. I then happened to see what was said about the Baptism in the Holy Spirit. I believed it, and Jesus baptized me in the Holy Spirit! At that moment I was filled with a joy which I had never felt before. I felt like walking on clouds. For the first time in my life I felt peace. Tremendous peace!"

A charming lady in her sixties, mother of four children, regularly attends prayer group meetings. She also holds a prayer group in her own home. One of her sons—a famous entertainer—a few years ago, together with his wife, had experienced the charismatic renewal. This also led his father, mother, other members of his family, and many others to a fuller spiritual life. The mother describes her experience of the Baptism in the Holy Spirit as follows: "My husband and I were hungry, undernourished Christians, who knew very little about the Holy Spirit because we had not gotten any teaching in that subject. But when we saw the change which took hold of our elder son—the entertainer—and his wife, we understood that there was something deeper and more in religion than what we had

117

gotten through our 'traditional teachings.' In spite of seeing the change in our boy and his family, we thought that they theologically were wrong, and we decided to start to study the Scriptures. We prayed to God to lead us through His Word so we would be able to find passages to lead our boy and his wife back to 'the true teachings of the church.' But we also prayed, 'Father if there is more to receive than what we have been led to believe through our traditional way of Bible interpretation, let us see it perfectly clearly because we do not want to miss any of the blessings you have for your children.' We studied and we prayed, and after one and a half years we were convinced that God had more to give. So we came to God in prayers and asked for more. My husband was baptized in the Holy Spirit one Monday morning in October, a little more than two years ago; and I, the following morning.

"I was still sleeping and had a dream in which I saw an altar with cloven tongues of fire and Jesus standing at the altar. When my dream disappeared, I woke up and was ready to jump for joy. Never before had I felt such euphoria. And I was expressing my praises to the Lord in another language! Then I went to sleep again, in a deep and peaceful sleep.

"Earlier I was a person who was always worried about everything. If there was nothing to worry about, I was able to construct something. But now I have left everything to the Lord, and He has given me peace instead. My health status has improved since I experienced the Baptism in the Holy Spirit. Earlier I never felt a hundred percent healthy, and on doctor's orders I had to take medicines of different kinds. I do not need medicines any more.

"I had been taught that no such thing as Baptism in the Holy Spirit existed; there was no speaking in tongues in our time, no spiritual gifts now—only the fruits of God's Spirit. The miracles ceased with the apostles, etc. So they said. But if you wake up in the middle of a dream and speak in tongues, then you believe. When you see healings take place, then you believe all this is real and that it is for us here and now."

Her husband, also in his sixties, describes what happened to him as follows: "My wife and myself have been members of a certain church for many, many years. We have always been careful to read our Bibles and to go to church. About four years ago we started to study the Bible to be able to quote Scriptures when trying to convince our son and his wife, who both had been baptized in the Holy Spirit, how wrong they were. We wanted to convert them from what we believed to be unbiblical.

"One and a half years passed without anything specific happening. Our son and his family were still burning for the Lord and their examples had meant much to many, but we still had difficulties in believing that what they had was from God. Then something happened on a perfectly normal Monday morning. I had slept well all night and felt calm and harmonious. I was not troubled about anything. I did not feel hurried and had no crisis of any kind in my life. I was only happy and content after a good night's rest. I had shaved, had my breakfast, read the morning paper, studied my Bible, and knelt to pray, exactly like hundreds of other mornings. My wife was still sleeping. I prayed to the Lord to give me everything He had in store for me. A feeling of elation came over me. For a moment I held it back because of fear. But I did let the happiness and elation come through. I got a peace greater than anything I had felt in my entire life. I had been filled with God through His Holy Spirit."

THE BAPTISM IN THE HOLY SPIRIT
NO RESULT OF HYPNOSIS

People who have criticized the Baptism in the Holy

Spirit and speaking in tongues have said that it is a product of suggestion attained in big crowds of people or of picking up certain expressions which a minister shouts in the ears of his victims, which phrases the victims later repeat. Is there an argument against such statements better than testimonies like these? Is it possible that the Baptism in the Holy Spirit can be free from all human influence and emotional mass suggestions? No mass suggestions but their own studies of the Scriptures compared with simple healthy testimonies in word and deed have been pointers which have made people aware of these blessings and their need for them.

"Our daughter first had this experience. I accompanied her to meetings at the Chapel, and I saw the love and happiness which these people had. This made me pray for the Baptism in the Holy Spirit," one lady in her late middle age said. She continues, "I started to study what the Bible says about the Baptism in the Holy Spirit. I attended prayer meetings, and soon I experienced the same blessings of the spirit as my daughter had had earlier."

"My wife had the charismatic experience first. She did not say anything to me, because she knew that I was negative to this. But I saw the change that took place in her, the happiness that radiated from her, so I asked her what had happened. She told me that she had really met God, the Holy Spirit. I then realized that this was real. I also started to pray for the Baptism, and only a short period afterwards I received the Spirit," a man who is a member of an Episcopal church told us.

Entirely other groups—consisting of the young coming directly from addiction to drugs and alcohol—are also baptized in the Holy Spirit these days, usually at the same time that the individual comes to the Lord for salvation. They get it all in one wrapping, including speaking in tongues.

A young Catholic girl tells us, "A brother to my husband told us convincingly about Jesus and how He could come in and rule our lives if we invited Him. We had just discovered what a perfectly meaningless life we lived. To a high degree drugs had contributed to make everything unbearable. My husband and I talked this over one day when we were sober, and we decided to try and see if what my brother-in-law had testified about was true. Without expecting anything to happen, we asked Jesus to take hold of our lives. In the very moment we prayed that prayer, both of us felt a terrific happiness, and as soon as we possibly could we went over to my brother-in-law to tell him what had happened. What good news! Beaming with happiness he congratulated us and praised the Lord with us. At the same time he said that we also would experience the Baptism in the Holy Spirit. We were open for all God's blessings and prayed for the Baptism in the Spirit. We scarcely had finished our prayer before the Spirit of God fell over us."

PERSONAL PROBLEMS HAVE LED PEOPLE CLOSER TO THE LORD

Personal problems and tragedies have actually benefited people in desperation who have been looking for answers. A man told us how he had asked for special prayers for his alcoholic problems and how he succeeded in abstaining for three months but had started again. Then he was baptized in the Holy Spirit! He has not tasted any form of alcoholic beverage since! Neither has he during all this time since then—and it is more than a year ago—felt the slightest need for alcohol!

"I am thanking the Lord for this miracle," he says. "It is a real miracle which has taken place, and I am sure that without this I would still be an alcoholic. I *was* an alcoholic, but now I am free, completely free!!"

121

Problems with relatives, such as teen-age children using drugs, also have sometimes been the reasons for people to seek a deeper life in God, which in its turn has led to the charismatic experience. But the majority of the ones we met declared that their prayers to receive the Baptism in the Holy Spirit did not coincide in time with any period of personal problems. These people merely started to feel an inner need to more committedly and fully be able to express their natural religiosity.

AGE AND SEX DISTRIBUTION

Who are the people that come to the Chapel who in their turn are reflecting the population of the charismatic prayer groups in the city? Looking at sex as a variable we find less than 60 percent women and a little bit more than 40 percent men. The women are in the majority in all ages, above all in the ages between 40 and 59, where there are twice as many women as men. The excess number of women come more from the group "earlier married"—that is widows or divorced—than from the group "never earlier married." The number of "never earlier married" is the same for both women and men. It can also be mentioned that the relatively large number of divorced women mainly represents the ages 25-39.

The number of married women also exceeds the number of married men. This is caused by the fact that the men, even as charismatics, do not have time to participate as often as their wives, and the fact that many of the women "have not yet succeeded in winning their husbands to the Lord." Usually the women came to the Lord first. Several of the men we have talked to or who answered our questionnaire state that first their wives were saved and filled with the Spirit, and when the men saw the change which took place in their wives' lives, they also became interested and prayed for the same experience.

The average age is very low. About half are under 25 years of age. This is true for both sexes.

There is a seemingly self-explanatory and definitely observable fellowship between all ages. These people are brothers and sisters, sons and daughters, fathers and mothers in God. And how many young fathers and mothers their age! Here you will find sixty-year-old sons to twenty-year-old fathers!! This means that many young persons take responsibility for persons of all ages who have recently come to the Lord. It is inconceivable how fast some of these newly reborn grow into strong, supporting pillars in the kingdom of the Lord—a kingdom where nothing is impossible when it comes to spiritual growth and everything else!

The professional and academic schooling of these people covers a broad range. Most of them have graduated from high school. Many have a college degree—some a master's or even a doctor's degree. Several women have started college, but for one reason or another they have not graduated. The most common reason for this is marriage.

ALL EDUCATIONAL LEVELS— ALL PROFESSIONS

All educational levels are represented, and thereby all types of professions. We find bricklayers and construction workers, farmers, teachers, secretaries, engineers, businessmen, physicians, car mechanics, lawyers, and university, college, and high school professors, teachers, and students; and of course also housewives and persons who have already retired. The charismatic movement, as it is represented by the people coming to the Chapel, in its turn representing the prayer groups in the city where we have studied it, thus is encircling a wide range of social, economic, and educational groups.

BEING ABLE TO TAKE RESPONSIBILITY

How, then, did the experience of the Holy Spirit change these people's lives? There are three areas frequently referred to in the answers:

Number One is that the writings in the Bible have become more meaningful. Every day they find how verses in the Scriptures are applicable to real situations here and now.

Number Two is that they, just because of this, have a new openness and frankness in testifying about their experiences.

Number Three is that they all testify to experiences of spiritual growth in their own lives, referring to what St. Paul writes to the Galatians in the fifth chapter:

> But the fruit of the Spirit is love, joy, peace, longsuffering, gentleness, goodness, faith, meekness, temperance (GALATIANS 5:22, 23a).

It is, above all, love to other people which is indicated in testimony after testimony like these:

"I care more about other people."

"I have been filled with love for my fellowman."

"Earlier I chose my friends; now I love all."

"I have love, happiness, peace to a degree which I did not believe was possible to receive."

"I do not become so easily irritated as earlier. I have more patience."

A young man just out of military service, during which time he was baptized in the Holy Spirit, tells us the following: "The most fantastic thing is the love with which I was filled. For the first time in my life I was able to love everybody—even my sergeant."

There also are testimonies about how some have experienced increased success in their studies and professional

124

lives. Young people—earlier on drugs, coming from a philosophy where all are permitted to do whatever comes to their minds, such as quit work and drop out of school—have become functioning citizens again willing to accept responsibility. The ones who dropped out of school or who were not doing their best have got a new motivation and, therefore, a new interest leading to honest studies, which have resulted in good grades. Some have even become honor students! Businessmen and professionals willingly admit increased economic success.

OLD PLUS NEW FRIENDS

The Baptism in the Holy Spirit has meant changed relationships to persons in the immediate environment. Some voluntarily have gradually come to see their earlier friends socially less often because they have new interests and new social habits. They have instead met a broader range of new people with whom they have more in common than they ever had with their old friends. "We lost a few of our friends but the Lord gave us new, who love Jesus as we do." And "Earlier my circle of acquaintances consisted of only 'our social level,' but now I enjoy greater and deeper fellowship with my new prayer group friends from all social strata, and I see the others mainly to get an opportunity to testify about the Lord."

CHANGED SEXUAL BEHAVIOR

The charismatic experience has also changed sexual behavior. Natural instincts have come back. Homosexuality and other perversities, epidemic in their manner of grouping, belong to the past. These are normal people again. Many had lived a life torn by their sexual desires in constant situations of conflict between immediate skin satisfaction and a hunger to live a "clean" life. For them it is now, through grace, perfectly natural for sexual abstinence before marriage. This spontaneous desire for purity is characteristic of the charismatic movement. Their own previous experiences had obviously been totally unsatisfactory, no matter how much they had tried to explain their delinquent behavior with liberal "new moral" reasoning.

At the same time many married charismatics explain how much richer and more meaningful their sexual lives have become after their charismatic renewal. They claim that when their spiritual lives were functioning to a satisfactory capacity, then their bodies reached harmony.

The family life has also improved in other areas. There are examples of marriages which were saved through the parties' being baptized in the Holy Spirit—marriages which before one or both of the two met God through the Baptism of the Holy Spirit were in a real crisis situation. Both were ready to leave the other, but fell in love anew after having met God's love through the charismatic experience.

In marriages where the relations were already good, they testify to the fact that husband and wife came even closer to each other. They became more open and the communications between them improved. "After having become more aware of the 'order' in marriage, my husband has more willingly accepted his role as 'master,' husband, and father," several women say.

BETTER COMMUNICATIONS
BETWEEN GENERATIONS

The communications between parents and children have also improved. Parents have more patience with and time for their children. The children have more love and obedience for their parents. The feeling of kinship has increased.

"I loved them for the first time, and I could also show them love," a young girl says about her parents after she was baptized in the Holy Spirit.

"My relationship to my parents changed from hatred to love," a young man relates after his charismatic experience.

126

"I hated my mother-in-law, but Jesus set me free from all hatred when He baptized me in the Holy Spirit," a young housewife told us.

The examples of this unexplainable but transforming love of God are repeated many times in our interviews.

And now abideth faith, hope, charity, these three; but the greatest of these is charity (CORINTHIANS 13:13).

CHANGED SMOKING AND DRINKING HABITS

The experience of the Baptism in the Holy Spirit has also influenced those people's tobacco and alcoholic habits. Somewhat less than half of those interviewed—two out of three of the men and one out of three of the women—had smoked up until the day of their charismatic experience. Of these, all except one woman and two men have stopped smoking.

Concerning drinking habits, a little over half used alcoholic beverages before their experience of the Baptism in the Holy Spirit, somewhat more men than women. Four out of five of these—men and women alike—have stopped using all forms of alcoholic beverages! The remainder explain that they use alcoholic beverages to a much lesser extent and much more seldom than before.

RETAIN THEIR OLD MEMBERSHIPS

"Do the persons who have received the Baptism in the Holy Spirit in the charismatic renewal retain their memberships in their churches or do they have to join a church where the Baptism in the Holy Spirit is traditionally sought?" is a usual question.

In the population we have studied the preponderance of the ones who earlier in their lives were members of Baptist and Methodist churches now mainly attend the Chapel services, as if the Chapel were their new church home, while the members of Episcopal, Presbyterian, and Lutheran churches still mainly attend their own churches at the same time that they come as often as they can to the Chapel. But there are many Baptists, Methodists, and Church of Christ people in this group, too. Some do as follows on Sundays: First they attend an early service in their own church, and then they come to the Chapel at eleven o'clock; or they go to their regular church in the morning and to the Chapel in the evening!

"We attend our church where we are members and the Chapel for the fellowship in the Lord," as one woman expresses this phenomenon, the psychology behind which we will discuss later. However, we have never heard anyone in the Chapel or in Bible study or prayer groups ever say anything negative about other Christians or other churches. Neither have we heard anyone ask anybody to leave the churches where the priests or ministers are not open to the charismatic renewal. The charismatic movement leaves open doors to renewal everywhere within all churches and denominations, and seems to have reached most of them, if not all.

The majority of the people in the population we have studied who come to the Chapel and to the charismatic prayer groups thus retain their membership in their own churches where they serve in different capacities as Sunday School teachers, choir members, members of different committees, etc. The type of Christian faith which they have gotten through the charismatic experience is expressed through the enthusiasm with which they serve.

The charismatics are also able to give their recommendations in the choice of speakers for certain occasions in their churches. Doing this, many charismatics feel that they are allowed to play a role in furthering the messages about a richer spiritual life to their own church people, in a better way than if they had tried to explain their experiences themselves.

NEW DIMENSIONS OF LOVE IN
THE FAMILY OF CHURCHES

A singer who always attends the Chapel when in the city relates that she is often invited to sing in different churches and service clubs. There she often meets charismatic friends who had had a part in the invitation. But, even where she did not know anyone before, she found signs of the pronounced growth of the charismatic movement. Several times she was invited to sing for the nuns in a well-known convent. There she was fascinated by the love and enthusiasm which the charismatic movement had given to many of the nuns. In this renewal, Kathryn Kuhlman especially had meant a lot to them. The loved her Christ-centered testimonies, and they always saw Miss Kuhlman's TV program Sunday morning between masses, and sometimes went to her services in Pittsburgh. One of the assistant mother superiors had had a charismatic experience at such a service. This nun afterwards had started a charismatic prayer group in the convent—a prayer group open to the public. The testimonies filled with God's glory and the gifts of the Spirit in action which the sisters communicated to everyone were so precious, the singer felt, that they were worthy of being given in the Baptist church where she was a member. First, she invited the sisters to her home together with a Sunday School class of married couples in their younger middle age. All were taken by the sisters' testimonies; and in a prayer and testimony time concluding the evening, the class shared personal spiritual experiences with a new openness. All wanted to hear more, and they wanted to meet the sisters again soon. This led to an invitation in which the sisters were asked to come as soon as they possibly could to the downtown Baptist cathedral to give their testimonies. A few Sundays later they came. Old Baptist gray-haired gentlemen were crying with joy when they heard the beautiful things about the

129

Lord which the sisters had experienced in abundance, and already that Sunday morning before the "standard" morning service people had asked for special prayers. An ecumenical fellowship of great beauty! Catholic sisters laying hands on brothers and sisters on a Sunday morning in a downtown Baptist church!

The testimonies about what happened then and later in that church are filled with joy and love and a new understanding between Catholics and Protestants. The upwinds of the charismatic revival started to blow in renewal and salvation and an entirely new purposefulness and happiness in God's work.

In a Methodist church a Sunday School class is studying the subject, "The Holy Spirit." It consists of adult church members who are all interested in the Baptism of the Holy Spirit, but none of them have had that experience. The teacher of the class has a friend working at the same office where he does. This friend had testified to him about the charismatic experience. His friend, a civil engineer, and his wife, members of an Episcopal church, were invited to give their testimonies.

The wife first had the charismatic experience. The transformation in her life made such an impact on the husband that he also wanted this experience. The wife had been baptized while alone. She is a lively, outgoing person. He is somewhat reserved and careful with emotions. He was baptized in the Spirit under the laying on of hands in a lively Pentecostal meeting!

For the Sunday School class they now relate the changes which have taken place in their lives since they had the charismatic renewal. When they are through, everybody is moved; some even wipe tears from their eyes. One asks several questions, and this Episcopal couple explains the secrets of the Baptism in the Holy Spirit for their sisters and brothers, the Methodists. Judging from their touching desire for knowledge, it probably will not take long before members of this Sunday School class will also testify about their Baptism in the Holy Spirit.

LOYAL IN SPITE OF
SOME MISUNDERSTANDING

Most of the ones who have moved from their old churches have done so of free will, for instance because they have moved to the city or to another part of the city and then have started to go to the Chapel almost entirely, or because they are not feeling at home anymore in their old fellowships. Only very few have been asked to leave their old churches.

"My husband and I were simply advised to leave because our membership was withdrawn, with the motivation that 'our teachings' and 'the official teachings of the church' could not exist together," a gray-haired lady told us. "But the Lord has given love between each other anyway, so we can pray together, and we still attend the services almost every Sunday morning without the resentment of anybody. The spiritual fellowship is on another level than opinions on dogmatic questions."

The most negative view concerning the charismatic movement is coming from denominations of fundamentalistic faith. Certain signs, however, indicate a new attitude in these denominations' official publications. Many ministers as well as members of these denominations have experienced the charismatic renewal and many others are open to this movement. The newly Spirit-baptized like, most of all, to stay where they belong to be able to testify with their lives to others that there is a richer Christian life to live. They wait and pray that the Spirit of the Lord shall reach others also in their own churches for a richer spiritual harmony and growth.

Futhermore, many have not wanted to leave their churches in the lurch as these people are serving in different functions. Because they are loyal they have retained

131

their membership. We studied the number of church visits these people made before and after their charismatic experience. The results confirm our impressions. Among these, the number of church visits a week has not increased. Before their charismatic experience they were already such busy churchgoers that now they only have time to visit the Chapel now and then, besides all the services for which they already are "booked" in their own churches.

Among those who now mainly go to the Chapel and to prayer meetings the picture is different. From not going to church at all or only occasionally previously, and then only Sunday mornings, they now attend church or prayer meetings three to four times a week. In other words, the ones belonging to this group before their charismatic experiences were neither in function nor emotionally real members of a church, so they now feel that they are of more service to the Chapel to help and counsel some of the constantly many newly converted.

"Going to church" thus for the charismatics becomes a question of where, as a blessing to others, they would be able to serve the Lord best. "God, lead me so I may be used by You as Your servant wherever you want," is an often-prayed prayer.

The Baptism in the Holy Spirit enriches the trust in God's guidance of an individual person's life. The faith has deepened in a remarkable way in these people. They have more and more trust in the Lord and His almighty powers. There has been more thanksgiving and praise in the prayers. They feel that they can praise the Lord during all circumstances in life. They believe in the gifts of the Spirit in function here and now; they believe that miracles can happen through the Holy Spirit today—that they still live in the times of the ACTS.

In summary: The charismatics have a quite "mixed background" concerning earlier spiritual experiences—former drug addicts who never before or never since they were small children have attended a church; church members who have been indifferent for a long time and almost stopped attending church; and firm Christians who always have been staunch supporters of the church and regularly and often have attended. All have been touched by the charismatic movement.

They were tired of artificial stimulants and had sought God's help to be free. They were tired of tiring indifference and sought God's answer for a richer life through the Holy Spirit. The charismatic movement has reached all kinds of people in all churches and denominations and outside.

The newly Spirit-baptized show no tendencies to cause divisions within churches. They stay where they are and give new life to their own churches through increased personal and economic support.

Both women and men have been moved by the charismatic movement. The women most often are converted and baptized in the Spirit before their men. Because of this, the number of married women exceeds the number of married men. There are more widows than widowers and more divorced women than divorced men in our data. Among the young unmarried the distribution between the sexes is even.

All ages are represented. The numerous young people make the average age very low.

The charismatic movement as we have seen it reaches all social and economic groups as well as all educational and professional levels.

The charismatic experience has meant changed attitudes toward other people: better family relations, love to all people, peace, happiness, longsuffering. A renewal of spirit, mind, and body—they have with happiness been able to face the tasks of the everyday, healthy enough to give and take love, healthy enough to be loving, healthy enough to really function!

PART IV

Comments

CHAPTER 12

The First Day of Pentecost

And suddenly there came a sound from heaven as of a rushing, mighty wind, and it filled all the house where they were sitting. And there appeared unto them cloven tongues like as of fire, and it sat upon each of them. And they were all filled with the Holy Ghost, and began to speak with other tongues, as the Spirit gave them utterance (ACTS 2:2-4).

The outpouring of the Holy Spirit over the disciples and the rest who were assembled in the upper room on the first day of Pentecost was experienced as a literal fulfilling of the promise about the Spirit which Jesus had given to them.

And, being assembled together with them, commanded them that they should not depart from Jerusalem, but wait for the promise of the Father, which, saith he, ye have heard of me. For John truly baptized with water; but ye shall be baptized with the Holy Ghost not many days hence (ACTS 1:4-5).

For whom is the Baptism in the Holy Ghost?

137

For the promise is unto you and to your children, and to all that are afar off, even as many as the Lord our God shall call (ACTS 2:39).

Who are called? Everyone is called to receive Jesus Christ in faith, as their Saviour to forgiveness of their sins. This was the answer that Peter gave when they asked him what to do to be saved:

Repent, and be baptized every one of you in the name of Jesus Christ for the remission of sins, and ye shall receive the gift of the Holy Ghost (ACTS 2:38).

The Baptism of the Holy Spirit is accordingly not for certain selected people but for every believer.

And these signs shall follow them that believe; In my name shall they cast out devils; they shall speak with new tongues; they shall take up serpents; and if they drink any deadly thing, it shall not hurt them; they shall lay hands on the side, and they shall recover (MARK 16:17, 18).

The outpouring is also as the Apostle Peter said in his magnificent speech on the day of Pentecost, a fulfilling of the prophecy of Joel, when the Lord says,

And it shall come to pass afterward, that I will pour out of my spirit upon all flesh; and your sons and your daughters shall prophesy, your old men shall dream dreams, your young men shall see visions: And also upon the servants and upon the handmaids in those days will I pour out my spirit (JOEL 2:28, 29).

A clearly observable change took place in Peter on this historic first day of Pentecost. From shamefully despairingly having denied his Master and in fear having hidden himself behind bolt and bar, Peter preached frankly and fearlessly in the open with such a power that three thousand people believed.

Changes also took place in the attitudes of the rest of the apostles. From fear to frankness, from silence to fervent testifying, from despair to inspired enthusiasm to fulfill the Great Commandment:

Go ye therefore, and teach all nations, baptizing them in the name of the Father, and of the Son, and of the Holy Ghost: Teaching them to observe all things whatsoever I have commanded you: and lo, I am with you alway, even unto the end of the world. Amen
(MATTHEW 28:19, 20).

CHAPTER 13

The Second Day of Pentecost

On the first day of Pentecost the Christian fellowship was born. The disciples saw the call for missions in the great commandment in a gloriously new light. And as witnesses for Christ, they went out to preach about His Kingdom. The Acts give a thrilling and comprehensive account of this in a brilliant, scientific study by a physician, Luke. The history of the church enters a new epoch! The report by Luke covers part of the first century.

It is documented that the happenings of the first day of Pentecost constantly have been and are being repeated through the centuries ever since up to our day, however, with certain blanks in time and distinctness. Without claims of perfection, we are repeating in this chapter a few of the headlines in this history.

Montanus reported about Baptism in the Holy Spirit and speaking in tongues in the second century. His teaching, however, became the subject of discussions when his prophecies concerning the second coming of Jesus during his own lifetime did not prove to be correct.

Origin, who reports from the middle of the third century, and Chrysostom, from the middle of the fourth century, were both of the opinion that the report about speaking in tongues during their time was false. If tongues had ever been used, it was not for "their time" but had been specifically for the first day of Pentecost, they argued. The fact that these men discussed and talked about this matter, however, may also indicate that this miracle took place in their day.

Augustine says in the beginning of the fifth century: "We still do like the disciples, when they laid hands upon the Samaritans and prayed so the Holy Spirit fell on them. We expect the converts to speak in tongues."

From the Middle Ages there are accounts of tongues-speaking during evangelization pilgrimages, and many of the saints from these times were attributed with this miracle.

From the seventeenth century there are reports about outpourings of the Holy Spirit among the Huguenots. In the eighteenth century in England speaking in tongues occurred in a Catholic sect, so also in the Greek Orthodox church in Russia. In the beginning of this century a new wave of outpourings of the Holy Spirit grows in the United States among Greek Orthodox immigrants who had come from Russia. Some people from this group one day "accidentally" came in contact with a new Pentecostal wave which had originated in a Methodist Bible school. In 1907, among other countries, Sweden was reached by this Pentecostal revival.

From the beginning of the 1960's a new outpouring of the Holy Spirit is reported from places all over the world. This revival has been called the charismatic renewal, or neo-Pentecostalism. Accounts are given of charismatic revivals in Korea, Vietnam, Japan, the Philippines, Indonesia, India, Australia, Brazil, Argentina and other countries in South America, the Union of South Africa, Zaire and other countries in Africa, Israel, Portugal, the United States, Canada, Sweden, Norway, England, France, and Italy. Also from Hungary, Romania, the Soviet Union, and China, similar revival reports originate.

141

The miracle on the first day of Pentecost is thus repeated. THE SECOND DAY OF PENTECOST becomes an authentic continuation of the first day of Pentecost. One may also think of the second day of Pentecost as "the day afterwards," a day which is filled with doubt and hesitation for individuals when they are left alone with themselves. Later in this chapter we want to come back to this possible alternative. But first we will try to answer two questions: It is really written in the Bible that the miracles from the first day of Pentecost were repeated? How is the experience of the Baptism in the Holy Spirit described in the Bible?

In Acts, Luke gives four accounts of how persons were baptized in the Holy Spirit. At three of these four occasions, Luke describes that the Baptism in the Holy Spirit is accompanied by speaking in tongues. On the first day of Pentecost—

> And when the day of Pentecost was fully come, they were all with one accord in one place. And suddenly there came a sound from heaven as of a rushing mighty wind, and it filled all the house where they were sitting. And there appeared unto them cloven tongues like as of fire, and it sat upon each of them. And they were all filled with the Holy Ghost, and began to speak with other tongues, as the Spirit gave them utterance
> (LUKE 2:1-4).

In Cornelius' house—

> While Peter yet spake these words, the Holy Ghost fell on all them which heard the word. And they of the circumcision which believed were astonished, as many as came with Peter, because that on the Gentiles also was poured out the gift of the Holy Ghost. For they heard them speak with tongues, and magnify God
> (ACTS 10:44-46).

142

When St. Paul laid hands upon some disciples in Ephesus—

> And when Paul had laid his hands upon them, the
> Holy Ghost came on them; and they spake with
> tongues, and prophesied (ACTS 19:6).

At the fourth account—the one when Peter and John
prayed for some newly converted in Samaria—Luke does
not relate that speaking in tongues occurred as an immediate sign, but it is obvious that the Baptism in the Holy
Spirit on this occasion as well was manifested in some way
since Simon, the magician, *saw* that it was through the
laying on of hands by the apostles that the Spirit was out-
poured—

> Who, when they were come down, prayed for them,
> that they might receive the Holy Ghost: (For as yet
> he was fallen upon none of them: only they were bap
> tized in the name of the Lord Jesus.) Then laid they
> their hands on them, and they received the Holy
> Ghost. And when Simon saw that through laying on of
> the apostles' hands the Holy Ghost was given, he of-
> fered them money . . . (ACTS 8:15-18).

Augustine, for instance, in his interpretation of this passage takes for granted that the sign which Simon saw was
speaking in tongues.

What is speaking in tongues, this the most debated of all
the spiritual gifts? It is the speaking, the utterance, of words
and sentences which neither the one who speaks them nor
the one who listens to them usually understands. Because
of this, speaking in tongues has been called "the language
of angels." The Apostle Paul for instance uses this expression in 1 Corinthians 13:1—

> Though I speak with the tongues of men and of angels,

and have not charity, I am become as sounding brass, or a tinkling cymbal (1 CORINTHIANS 13:1).

Evaluated from a linguistic point of view, the speaking in tongues in most cases does not satisfactorily meet the criteria concerning either grammar or the number of words for an authentic language. However, exceptions are documented where completely uneducated persons in the Spirit have spoken known languages which they did not know before. One example of speaking in tongues in a known language is reported in this book, when modern Hebrew was spoken to a Jewish couple by a minister who had had Greek at the seminary, but not Hebrew.

Speaking in tongues is for the individual a "language for prayers," "a conversation from the heart with God for personal edification." It can also, accompanied by interpretation, be "a message from the Lord" to individuals or to the entire congregation.

What a person experiences in the moment when the Baptism in the Holy Spirit takes place has been described in many ways. One talks about a "strong inner release of happiness," about a "discharge of the soul," about an "electric shock from heaven," about "streams of living water," about a "healing of the memory," about a "healing of the mind," about a "cleansing out of guilt," etc. Some of these experiences describe a strong physical sensation which acquires a deep psychological meaning with evident endocrinal effects.

What happens later on their second day of Pentecost and the days and the years after that also has been described. With "cleansed minds" new dimensions for impressions open up for them. A newly awakened need to fill the now clean and empty room with God and more of God is manifested in the eagerness seen to study the Bible. They speak about a "hunger after God's word." The many new Bible study groups are a result of this. The importance of the hunger's being satisfied with "balanced food" is emphasized.

"Ask, and it shall be given you; seek, and ye shall find; knock, and it shall be opened unto you"
(MATTHEW 7:7).

The message of the Bible about peace, brotherhood, love, and joy fills their minds. They share beautiful programs for their lives with others. They do it with absolute trust that the people they talk to will understand how good and right this is. But then they become disappointed and understand that they need more and more of what Jesus told also his first disciples:

But ye shall receive power, after that the Holy Ghost is come upon you: and ye shall be witnesses unto me both in Jerusalem, and in all Judaea, and in Samaria, and unto the uttermost part of the earth (ACTS 1:8).

The Holy Spirit for the Christian becomes the well of power to be able to live day by day a witnessing, victorious life—a necessity in "the Holy war" against "sin,"

For we wrestle not against flesh and blood, but against principalities, against powers, against the rulers of the darkness of this world, against spiritual wickedness in high places (EPHESIANS 6:12).

They enter that war steadfastly leaning on this promise:

Verily, verily, I say unto you, He that believeth on me, the works that I do shall he do also; and greater works than these shall he do; because I go unto my Father
(JOHN 14:12).

145

Is no one to be found who later doubts his experience? Who feels like "the day afterwards"? Who on "the second day of Pentecost" feels like the day of Pentecost was unreal?

Referring to some of the case histories in this book, a "day-afterwards" or "immediately afterwards" feeling of doubt and hesitation, especially concerning the miracle of speaking in tongues, was felt by some. Such feelings obviously are not entirely unusual but are "natural", since our mood levels change. With their "intellect" they "understand" that they have experienced something authentic, but they doubt their feelings. But these feelings of a somewhat lowering of the level of enthusiasm are nothing compared with "the day-afterwards depressions" which these people felt while still "unsaved" and "without God." The spontaneous, unexplainable inner satisfaction and "setting-free feeling" which the Baptism in the Holy Spirit gave and continues to give day by day seems, in spite of whatever feelings there were the day afterwards, to leave so strong an impression that it is difficult to deny that something important happened and is happening with their whole person—body, mind, and spirit. Thus, we do not know one person having had an authentic charismatic experience who afterwards entirely denied everything. The experience of the Baptism in the Holy Spirit is of a deep, re-creating nature.

The miracle on the day of Pentecost was and is repeated! The second day of Pentecost was and is a continuation with the manifestation of the same miracles! Yes, the upwinds of the Holy Spirit are continuing to flow stronger and stronger! Oh, these warm winds of love!

CHAPTER 14

Questions and Answers in Summary

What we have described in this report are Sunday-and-weekday episodes in a spiritual revival. We have put together the "outward" frame for "inward" events and have tried to show a total picture. We have tried to take pictures of what people were before the revival reached them and what they became later on. The frame for the pictures has been described with concrete words as well as how these persons looked before and after they had the charismatic experience. For what happened "within" them "in their hearts" we have used abstract expressions—the ones which they used themselves.

ARE THE INVOLVED PEOPLE IN GENERAL?

Are the ones involved in this report people in general? Average people in the 1970's? We are not sure. Maybe they were average up to the day when they had the transforming religious experience which we have depicted. This experience was the requirement for their acceptance in this study. What we have looked at thus is a group of people who have all testified to a religious rebirth which has strongly altered and now influences their behavioral patterns. Many before that had, and some still have, difficult personal problems, for instance, ill health, need of counseling in their marriages, personal failures, children on drugs, sisters

147

and brothers and other relatives with trouble; others had not had any direct personal trials or difficulties. On the contrary, there were many who seemingly had been successful in most of what they had tried, if not in everything. But all these had one thing in common: they had all been touched by the new revival called the charismatic movement.

This revival during the last years has reached many persons in many places in society all over the world. It has reached people in the paintshops and in the company-president's office. It has given a new birth to students and professors at the universities. It has inspired teen-agers and retired people. It has blessed housewives and professional women—yes, it has filled old and young women and men with a new happiness and spiritual prosperity.

If the simple criteria on mental health which we stated in the introduction to this book—the ability to give and to receive love, the ability to be loving, the ability to perform some form of productive work, the ability to take responsibility—if these criteria are valid, then it is obvious that many of the ones we have depicted in this book have become healthier through the Baptism in the Holy Spirit. The book is filled with pictures about how just these qualities have become "theirs" through the Holy Spirit and also how their new open attitudes to life are kept and renewed through the Spirit. The book is a testimony about how these people are much more sensitive and loving toward others than before their charismatic experience, how their marriages, including sexual lives, have deepened and become more harmonious, how the many young have been able to wait with sexual relations until after their marriages, how they have matured to new codes for moral responsibilities, and how their new behavior and attitudes give and have given them a happiness of new, unforeseen dimensions.

Living in the Spirit gives renewal of the feeling of

"streams of living waters deep within," something they never before experienced in connection with religious practice. The Baptism in the Holy Spirit has been the cause of an emotional disentanglement, of a new openness, and at the same time, of a new intellectual activity. They understand, see, and know that a fundamental change has taken place. They have become "new people." They know! No wonder that on the second day of Pentecost they feel happy in general and tell people about what has happened to them. They consider what has happened a miracle which no one can take from them. The miracle is repeated day by day. They receive again and again power to become witnesses. They know that they speak "the angels' language" when they are alone, and they have understood the meaning in the Word,

But thou, when thou prayest, enter into thy closet, and when thou hast shut thy door, pray to thy Father which is in secret; and thy Father which seeth in secret shall reward thee openly (MATTHEW 6:6).

The charismatics are not seen running around scaring people by speaking in tongues. Their openness is on another level, just as their emotional disentanglement is. When people get baptized in the Holy Spirit, they become new, free persons. The fact is that there is no place for ecstasy. Never have we seen the experience of the Baptism in the Holy Spirit preceded by prayers with many words which in an emotional way would lead to a moment of ecstasy, when the Baptism in the Holy Spirit is expected to take place. No, they claim without hesitation God's promises in the Bible concerning the Baptism in the Holy Spirit and see immediate results. This attitude is very genuine. The charismatic movement is characterized by indisputable honesty and reality.

WILL THIS REVIVAL LAST?

Will this revival last? Is this a true movement of God, or is it an outburst of epidemic, disuniting, emotional fanaticism?

Many consider—and they seem to be the majority—that the charismatic renewal really is from God and that it even fulfills the prophecy about the power of the Spirit poured out over people as Joel describes it. The young should be given power to be victorious and be blessed by visions about their role in the growth of the Kingdom of God. The old should feel God's mighty protecting nearness and care during lonely years of aging.

Others say, "O.K., in this renewal most of the converts are real people and God is with them, but 'the Jesus movement' is not real. Among the Jesus-people, religion is 'only' a new way to be high and to avoid the truth about reality," such people say.

Still others take a more hesitating stand and say, as Gamaliel, "If this is a work by people, it will fall, but if it is from God it will last."

And now I say unto you, Refrain from these men, and let them alone: for if this counsel or this work be of men, it will come to nought: But if it be of God, ye cannot overthrow it; lest haply ye be found even to fight against God (ACTS 5:38, 39).

Whatever stand one may take concerning the charismatic movement, one has to admit that it, for about five years, has had an apparent epidemic growth. The cause of this is the personal, religious engagement which every charismatic shows. They do not keep "the blessings" to themselves, but tell them everywhere—at home, at work, in school, among friends. The experience of the Holy Spirit seems to color these people's lives, wherever they live and whichever type of status they may have. They testify about what has been and what is happening everywhere, always. This testifying by all has meant that this revival probably is more of a laymission movement than any earlier revival.

A dominance by the leaders becomes impossible in this general priesthood which does not sidestep the fulltime workers in the vineyard—the priests and the ministers:

> Then saith he unto his disciples, The harvest truly is plenteous, but the labourers are few; Pray ye therefore the Lord of the harvest, that he will send forth labourers into his harvest (MATTHEW 9:37, 38).

As long as this total engagement lasts and their holy enthusiasm remains, so long the revival will continue to grow. In the movement when they slow down and are content with only watching "taken territories" in an outward and inward sense, the growth of the charismatic movement ceases. But of slowing down in praising the Lord we have seen nothing. On the contrary! The movement is growing faster and faster, and the enthusiasm in these people taken individually seems to grow with their increasingly richer personal experiences of God's presence in the everyday world.

A REVIVAL OF LOVE

People with different theological languages now speak the same language. People who have not understood each other now do so out of kinship in the Spirit. The great miracle of the first day of Pentecost, to hear their own language spoken, is repeated on the second day of Pentecost throughout history into our day. The people in the charismatic movement understand others and each other better through the flowing love which is manifested everywhere. The wave of revival has reached out to all. Cath-

olics, Lutherans, different groups of Baptists, other Protestants—yes, all now speak in understanding with humble
mildness and admiration about and with one another. They
talk more lovingly about all, including the ones who are
"outside." So warm and generous, so great and overflowing,
is the love.

The humility before God and the willingness to be used
as HIS instrument in love for others has brought about a
"revolution" concerning traditional theological conceptions.
The charismatics do not discuss differences but praise the
Lord for the similarities. They no longer talk about old
denominational quarrels; they talk about the fact that they
are "relatives." They no longer talk about owning spiritual
gifts; they talk about the possibilities of being used as a
channel in service to the Lord for a special gift, but also
for whatever gift the Lord chooses to use them for. They
talk about the variety of spiritual gifts and testify to having
experienced how anybody, despite all outward circumstances, can be used by God as His instrument for any
gift. All to the glory of God and only to the glory of God!

The charismatic experience has set people free from
hang-ups. It has meant a journey into the reality. People
have been liberated from traditional roles. They have become eager to give themselves in service for others in love.

"But he that is greatest among you shall be your servant
(MATTHEW 23:11).

We have thus, with origin in and references to an old
charismatic movement, studied a new, or rather an old
revival movement which has continued into a new time,
and there flared up in different corners of the world among
other people. What has astonished us is how independent
of time, place, and other environmental factors the charismatic movement throughout the years seems to be in its

experiences and features. We find in different places all over the world, as well as in Sweden, the same manner of praising the Lord now as back in Sweden fifty and twenty-five years ago—the same changes in people's behavioral patterns, the same longing for purity, the same love and the same faith, the same steady growth in the kingdom of God, and lastly the same genuine, normal, healthy people.

The same and yet so much new: it is as if the new wave of the charismatic movement has from the beginning been able to enter immediately what it had taken the old many years to "ripen" into—openness to all denominations and all sorts of people, little emphasis on dogmatic discussions, humility when it comes to criticism, and great love to all. Isolationism and sectarianism have come to an end, and so has loneliness in the middle of a church service and between church services, through an out-flowing love of which all feel more obvious participation and experiences than ever.

"These things I command you, that ye love one another (JOHN 15:17).

These words by Jesus perhaps have been observed to a greater extent in our day than ever before. They love one another because they feel and understand more than ever before that they form a family. We all are sisters and brothers! The truth in that characteristic is easy to establish sociologically—the psychological effect as well.

They even say that God is in such a hurry these last days that He seems to have "forgotten" certain theological concepts. In other words, people are baptized in the Holy Spirit, not because they follow certain dogmatic ideas and rules, but for Grace alone.

The risk to become "overspiritual" has more and more disappeared in this revival where God uses whomever He chooses, one or several or all gathered together, or different persons every time. The risk for "dead" churches is eliminated when spontaneous participation by ministers and laymen is part of the picture—even in the middle of the liturgy.

Medically the new spontaneity and activity among the charismatics perhaps can be explained by the fact that when a person really is happy and harmonious, the endocrine glands finally function to capacity. "It is healthy to be saved," as the old Pentecostal preacher in Sweden said.

A religious manifestation which within Christianity is called "Baptism in the Holy Spirit" and which expresses a new beginning of a richer spiritual life thus has occurred throughout the centuries. The manifestation of this new life in the Holy Spirit in the persons who have been touched by it has led, for instance, to "changes in behavioral patterns," "healing of the memory," and "new health." There is a multitude of similar testimonies.

How is a scientific hypothesis proven? Through repeated unbiased experiments leading to the same result. Several reports about changes in people's lives through absolutely spontaneous charismatic experiences seem to support that it is impossible to shake off this phenomenon as being strange. On the contrary! The possibility for personal, including spiritual, growth of an individual through maximal religious development, therefore, has great public health interest.

P. S.
Warm Winds of Love

P. S.
Warm Winds of Love

The careful reader of this report understands by now
that "Warm Winds of Love" is the best name we could
find for the new powers a man receives when he applies in
his life Christ's words: "A new commandment I give unto
you, Love one another." This is exactly what happens in
all corners of the world today.

"The summer church," the enthusiastic outreach program for evangelization of the soon one thousand years
old Swedish Lutheran church, has installed its microphones
and amplifiers on a street corner one busy Saturday morning downtown in a Swedish city near the Arctic Circle.

About ten girls and boys, some in shirts with Christian
symbols on them, sing for shoppers and others who stop
for a moment or two to listen to the beloved old songs
about Jesus Christ, the name above all names, the name
through which "the pearly gates will open." These young
people are Lutherans, but they could as well have been
Southern Baptists, Methodists, or Assembly of God members. It is the same message, the same songs, the same faith,
the same hope, the same love, which they proclaim.

There he is as songleader—the 22-year-old boy whom we
know well from the beginning of this report. What has
happened to him since the last time we saw him? Great
things! It would take hours to describe everything in its
minute detail. But the most important features in his testimony are these: Before, he had liked to drink and to swear
and to pretend. He pretended to be an intellectual, a sophisticated, independent student. The alcohol intoxicated
him, gave him "courage," so he sang more hoarsely and

picked more diffuse and wild and complicated chords on his guitar. His songs were about how difficult everything was. It was "the in thing" to be sad and drink and complain.

"How heavy and hard and terrible it was for everyone who had to work for a living," they said. "What a generation of people addicted to working! Nowadays things are much better," they continued, "much better." They were members of a new generation, a generation which could free itself of hard work, a generation which did not need "to prostitute itself" to work for a living, a generation which could sleep in and always make late mornings. He pretended to be an intellectual of this breed!

He had lived this kind of nonsense and alcohol-intoxicated philosophy up until the moment he met Jesus Christ, who told him: "A new commandment I give unto you—love them all: the hardhat workers, the company presidents, and the girls in the checkout counters in your grocery store—every one of them!!"

After he understood these words, everything beautiful started to happen. He did not need beer or any other alcoholic drinks anymore, even if people wanted him to have a drink again.

Is this commandment about love for your fellowman really something worthwhile? "I think it is bluff altogether," said a so-called tough student, a former friend of his, one day. "Where is this love when you need it most? Come on, a couple of drinks would do you good." This former friend wanted him to fall, but he knew much better. He knew that the real bluff was to be found in mood-changing drugs, including alcohol and beer!

"Come on!" And they were on their way!! This "Big Daddy" saw. Big Daddy is a somewhat older Christian who always seems to be "at hand" when help is needed. Big Daddy said, "I want to talk to you. Tell me everything if you need to, but do not numb yourself with anesthetics!! You deserve better!"

What a difficult moment. But what a stream of happiness it gave to be able to refrain from drinks that day!!

He woke up quite early the next morning and started to read the Scriptures. It sounds heavy—a twenty-two-year-old boy reading his Bible early in the morning. What happened was that this boy found that the Scriptures were about him. He found many passages which were directly applicable to his situation day by day. He started to love people just as the Master had said. He was able to look at girls and love them as friends. He could look at women and men as sisters and brothers and close relatives. He found sisters in eighty-year-old ladies and brothers in boys who were eight.

He had found a functioning communion with the motto "LOVE ONE ANOTHER," and at his baptism in a Southern Baptist church, soaked with the baptistry water, he jubilantly hugged the minister! People laughed in love, unconstrained, as the water splashed off of the two of them.

His coming to the Lord thus changed him completely. He felt peace and balance; he was able to live a new kind of life. He stopped smoking, drinking, using drugs, and hunting around without a meaning. He has a new long-term goal and a role for his activities day by day: he wants to tell everybody in the entire world what is happening to him, and to explain it from the Scriptures. So he has started to study theology instead of philosophy. He enrolled in an interdenominational Bible school. What a blessing!

Now two years later he is standing here with his guitar as songleader in an outreach program in the Swedish Lutheran church. It is a summer job. When school starts this fall, he is going back to study. Soon he will graduate as a minister. His friends in "the summer church" say that he has been an instrument in leading them into a deeper life with the Lord, giving them not only new songs, but a new meaning in the singing: "Not by the power nor by the might of men, it shall be done, but by my Spirit says the Lord, but by my Spirit." The leaders of the outreach program say, "Without the Spirit of the Lord, the Spirit we saw living in our songleader, everything would have been entirely in vain.

"We wanted to do it ourselves. But we now understand that God was able to do it through us. We prayed together and everything was changed, because we were changed and believed in what we were doing. We suddenly understood the reality of the Lord!"

During the summer many came to the Lord; some were healed; some started in their prayers to speak the language of the angels, very naturally, just as a continuation of the ancient language of the church—a language filled with new words for love and victory. They said, "Remarkable! It is functioning! What is written about Love between people is functioning!! Here and now we feel the warm winds of Love!!!"

Just the same thing happened on a similar outreach program sponsored by a Baptist church. The 22-year-old songleader and his brother had been especially invited to participate. The outreach week was filled with house calls, visits to supermarkets and plants; and many services were held on the streetcorners. The same songs, the same methods, the same objectives, the same Spirit—everything was just the same as in the Lutheran summer program. No difference! The presence of the Lord was felt strongly and deeply. These two boys do not know the different traditions of the two churches. They do not know how it "ought to be." They have never before attended "prayer meetings" in their homeland. But they felt exactly the same "religious miracle" in both these denominations as when they had met God in quite another part of the world. The same way of worshipping the Lord in His temples! The same Spirit of Love! The same happiness and warmth! The same certainty of Gods' presence every day. No difference!! Warm upwinds of love made people "sail" everywhere!

They had experienced the same miracle in a special sense sometime earlier during the summer. It was when they worked as personnel in the cafeteria-tent at an Assembly of God summer meeting. They worked close to the people. They liked the food and the way people communicated with one another—so relaxed and good during the meals, and when they met between services, and in the evenings after the services. The sessions were filled with the presence of the Lord. What happened could not be explained in any other way than THIS IS GOD'S LOVE!

One question up for deliberation in the convention was "Evangelization." The twenty-two-year-old boy wanted to say something about that. He knew many who wanted to be set free from heavy burdens, but they did not know how. There was no fear and no hesitation within him when he stood up to speak—speak to a crowd of 10,000 in the giant tent-church. He said, "Before we will be able to make others Christ's disciples, we have to be disciples ourselves. Jesus said, 'Follow me!' When they followed him, he taught them above all one important lesson: love one another! He said that this was his new commandment. Evangelization, thus, is a declaration of love. It was this love which I felt when I came to Him. I felt 'the revolution of love,' and I am a completely new man through these warm winds of love."

In the daily press it was said about this session of the convention that God's power was present in a visible way. The power of love is strong!! It is that power which is the upwind, and in this upwind many have felt "strength

161

under their wings." People who did not even know that they had spiritual wings have felt the power and tried them, and now they fly new dimensions of their inner selves. They are new!!

We followed the personalities presented in this report for months—in some cases, more than two years. We followed them in their daily lives, at work and at leisure, at home and away from home. We followed them Sundays and weekdays to their churches and chapels, to prayer meetings and Bible studies and gatherings, and out to the street corners. We saw them in perspiring work, in victory and failure; we saw them in silent tears and in contagious laughter, in holy devotion and relaxed rest. We shared their bread and potatoes and salads. We saw their love, love expanding far outside their immediate circles, and we understood from the new way they lived that they really believed.

Without names and in only short snapshots of their lives, they have passed by in this book. They are here because we understood that their songs were expressing triumph, even if the words of the songs dealt with just one step at a time: "Every step Jesus leads me," "Only one day, a moment at a time," one moment at a time in victory and in difficulties.

The triumph was in their will to be led by the Master, who once said and is still saying, "A new commandment I give unto you—Love one another—" in everything. Up above all boundaries and shortcomings they were carried by these warm winds of love!

DATE DUE

#47-0108 Peel Off Pressure Sensitive